DOUBLE PORTION
The Miracles Of Elisha

Tom Akers

AFF
Publications
www.affp.1church4u.com

All rights reserved.

Published By:

Tom Akers

Seminole, Oklahoma

USA

www.affp.1church4u.com

admin@1church4u.com

All scripture quotations in this book are from the King James Version of the Bible.

ISBN:9798573471839

Contents

1. The Schools of the Prophets 5

2. Parting Of The Waters 18

3. God Is Not Mocked 30

4. Living In The Shadow 42

5. The Multiplier 56

6. Birth And Death 71

7. Deliverance From Another Quarter 87

8. The Walking Dead 102

9. Forsaken Glory 115

10. Swimming Lessons 127

11. The Windows Of Heaven 143

12. Double Famine 161

13. Empty Shoes 176

DOUBLE PORTION
The Miracles Of Elisha

Lesson One

The Schools of the Prophets

As children of the Living God Jesus Christ we all desire a double portion of the anointing power of God. Over the next few weeks we are going to study about the "Miracles of Elisha." The Prophet Elisha was blessed with a double portion and the mantle of Elijah when he was carried away to heaven in a chariot of fire. These lessons will bless you with insights from a prophet who had a double portion bestowed upon him. It is always so exciting to see God perform miracles in our lives so that all men can be drawn to the foot of the cross. As the church of the Living God we must have a hunger in our hearts to see the gifts working in our churches. 1 Corinthians 12:28-31 *"And God hath set some in the church, first apostles, secondarily prophets, thirdly teachers, after that miracles, then gifts of healings, helps, governments, diversities of tongues. Are all apostles? are all prophets? are all teachers? are all workers of miracles? Have all the gifts of healing? do all speak with tongues? do all interpret? But covet earnestly the best gifts: and yet shew I unto you a more excellent way."* So let us study about the "Miracles of Elisha" so that we will have a burning desire to be used as a worker of miracles!

Scripture Text

1 Samuel 19:20-23 *"And Saul sent messengers to take David: and when they saw the company of the prophets prophesying, and Samuel standing as appointed over them, the Spirit of God was upon the messengers of Saul, and they also prophesied. 21 And when it was told Saul, he sent other messengers, and they prophesied likewise. And Saul sent messengers again the third time, and they prophesied also. 22 Then went he also to Ramah, and came to a great well that is in Sechu: and he asked and said, Where are Samuel and David? And one said, Behold, they be at Naioth in Ramah. 23 And he went thither to Naioth in Ramah: and the Spirit of God was upon him also, and he went on, and prophesied, until he came to Naioth in Ramah."*

Definition of Naioth

OT:5121 A habitation or dwelling place of the company of the prophets in the time of Samuel.

Sons Of The Prophets

A study of Elisha would not be complete if we did not study about the Sons of the Prophets, because Elisha was chosen as their leader after the death of Elijah. 2 Kings 2:15 *"And when the sons of the prophets which were to view at Jericho saw him, they said, The spirit of Elijah doth rest on Elisha. And they came to meet him, and bowed themselves to the ground before him."* From all the information we can glean from the Word of God, we conclude that in modern day terminology the Sons of the Prophets were students at the Schools of the Prophets. The very first mention of these schools has the Prophet Samuel as the head of them. The name for the place where the School of the Prophets resided in Ramah was Naioth. We later see the Prophet Elijah and then Elisha as the leaders of the schools. We see the terms company and band being used to let us know that they were organized groups with leaders or teachers.

The Prophets

The first person referred to as a prophet was Abraham. Genesis 20:7 "*Now therefore restore the man his wife; for he is a prophet, and he shall pray for thee, and thou shalt live: and if thou restore her not, know thou that thou shalt surely die, thou, and all that are thine.*" There are two things we can glean from this verse. As a result of the relationship that Abraham had with God, he was considered a prophet by God and God was looking out for his welfare. Also he was someone who talked to God in prayer and God answered his prayers. We are not alone, God is watching over us and cares about our everyday problems. Today as righteous men and women we have a promise that God hears and answers our prayers. James 5:16 "*Confess your faults one to another, and pray one for another, that ye may be healed. The effectual fervent prayer of a righteous man availeth much.*" What we must remember is that God does not always give us the answer we expect. But God always has our best interest at heart and will do what is best for us. Brother James also warns us that God is not a magic genie that will give you anything you ask for even if it will harm you. James 4:3 "*Ye ask, and receive not, because ye ask amiss, that ye may consume it upon your lusts.*" But we are assured the way to get what we ask for every time is ask for what God wants. When our goals, desires and plans are to do what God has called us to do, then God will make a way. The beautiful thing about trusting in God is that he know ways to do things that we do not know of and cannot see. So when the path in front of you is blocked and you must take a detour, just realize it was God's intended route all along.

Moses is the next big prophet that the Word of the Lord speaks about. There is no one who can doubt that Moses was a prophet who heard from God. From the ten plagues in Egypt to the building of the tabernacle in the wilderness, Moses was a prophet who spoke to God face to face. Moses even prophesied about the coming of the messiah. Deuteronomy 18:15-18 "The LORD thy God will raise up unto thee a Prophet from the midst of thee, of thy brethren, like unto me; unto him ye shall hearken; According to all that thou desiredst of the LORD thy God in Horeb in the day of the assembly, saying, Let me not hear again the voice of the LORD my God, neither let me see this great fire any more, that I die not. And the LORD said unto me, They have well spoken that which they have spoken. I will raise them up a Prophet from among their brethren, like unto thee, and will put my words in his mouth; and he shall speak unto them all that I shall command him." Moses gave us the insight that a prophet had the Spirt of the Lord upon him. This was not the case for the rest of the children of Israel. Numbers 11:29 *"And Moses said unto him, Enviest thou for my sake? would God that all the LORD'S people were prophets, and that the LORD would put his spirit upon them!"* But even Moses did not hold a monopoly on the office of prophet. There was a need for other prophets to work under him. The work of the Lord because so overwhelming that God had Moses pick out seventy prophets to lead the people. Numbers 11:24-25 *"And Moses went out, and told the people the words of the LORD, and gathered the seventy men of the elders of the people, and set them round about the tabernacle. And the LORD came down in a cloud, and spake unto him, and took of the spirit that was upon him, and gave it unto the seventy elders: and it came to pass, that, when the spirit rested upon them, they prophesied, and did not cease."* Here is another example of the anointing of God flowing through the man of God to those who are called to help in the work of the Lord. There is one thing we need to grasp as we study about the Schools of the Prophets, God has a pastor he has placed in your church and the anointing flows through the office of the pastor. There are no lone rangers in the Kingdom of God. Every ministry works out of the church with God mandated accountability.

Next we find ourselves looking at the Prophet Samuel. Between Moses and Samuel Israel passed through a diversity of leaders in its history. Few characters appeared who made much of a change or left much of an impression on its political and religious life. No great prophet comes forth until Samuel is called. He is the last and the greatest of the judges, the end of the old order of things and the beginning of the new and the transition from the theocracy to the monarchy. He is the one God chose to be the reorganizer of Israel, politically and religiously. He filled the office of priest, prophet and judge. God used him to anoint the first two kings of Israel. Political and religious Israel is revolutionized in his day. During his life we find the existence and probably the beginning of the Schools of the Prophets (band or company of the sons of the prophets). The Prophet Jerimiah gave Samuel the same standing as Moses. Jeremiah 15:1 *"Then said the LORD unto me, Though Moses and Samuel stood before me, yet my mind could not be toward this people: cast them out of my sight, and let them go forth."* King David tells us that Samuel got his prayers answered just like Moses did. Psalms 99:6 *"Moses and Aaron among his priests, and Samuel among them that call upon his name; they called upon the LORD, and he answered them."* There is evidence to suggest that he had schools in several different cities and could have visited them on his yearly rounds. 1 Samuel 7:16-17 *"And he went from year to year in circuit to Bethel, and Gilgal, and Mizpeh, and judged Israel in all those places. And his return was to Ramah; for there was his house; and there he judged Israel; and there he built an altar unto the LORD."*

Locations

Now that we have established that we have Biblical backing for the concept of Schools of the Prophets, let's look at what we know about them. There are seven things we know about the Sons of the Prophets: 1 organized in bands, companies or schools, 2 had several schools in different locations, 3 had several leaders throughout the years, 4 had teaching and active involvement in worship, 5 were full time students, 6 was supported by the offerings of the people, 7 stayed in the same dwelling.

Ramah

Ramah was the birthplace and home of Samuel. After he made his yearly circuit, he return was to Ramah, for there was his house; and there he judged Israel: and he built there an altar unto Jehovah.   When Saul was in pursuit of David, he fled, and escaped, and came to Samuel to Ramah, they saw the company of prophets prophesying, and Samuel standing as head over them. We find that three successive sets of messengers from Saul prophesied as soon as they come into contact with the sons of the prophets and also that Saul himself finally comes down and prophesied. At this place was probably the original school of the prophets as founded by Samuel. (1 Samuel 19:20-23)

Bethel

We have no definite information that a school existed in Bethel in Samuel's day. But the Word of God tells us that men were going there to worship God. 1 Samuel 10:3-7 *"Then shalt thou go on forward from thence, and thou shalt come to the plain of Tabor, and there shall meet thee three men going up to God to Bethel, one carrying three kids, and another carrying three loaves of bread, and another carrying a bottle of wine: And they will salute thee, and give thee two loaves of bread; which thou shalt receive of their hands. After that thou shalt come to the hill of God, where is the garrison of the Philistines: and it shall come to pass, when thou art come thither to the city, that thou shalt meet a company of prophets coming down from the high place with a psaltery, and a tabret, and a pipe, and a harp, before them; and they shall prophesy: And the Spirit of the LORD will come upon thee, and thou shalt prophesy with them, and shalt be turned into another man. And let it be, when these signs are come unto thee, that thou do as occasion serve thee; for God is with thee."* We know that it had sons of a prophets dwelling there during the reign of Jeroboam. 1 Kings 13:11 *"Now there dwelt an old prophet in Bethel; and his sons came and told him all the works that the man of God had done that day in Bethel: the words which he had spoken unto the king, them they told also to their father."* While Elijah and Elisha were on their way to the place of translation for Elijah, The sons of the Prophets that were at Bethel came forth to Elisha, and said unto him, knowest thou that Jehovah will take away thy master from thy head, today? And he said, Yea, I know it; hold ye your peace. After his return from the east of the Jordan, Elisha went up from thence to Bethel. Probably with the express purpose of reporting to the sons of the prophets his sad experience in the loss of his Elijah.

Gilgal

Samuel commanded Saul to go to Gilgal. 1 Samuel 10:8 *"And thou shalt go down before me to Gilgal; and, behold, I will come down unto thee, to offer burnt offerings, and to sacrifice sacrifices of peace offerings: seven days shalt thou tarry, till I come to thee, and shew thee what thou shalt do."* Then we find the prophesyings of Saul among the sons of the prophets in the neighborhood of Gibeah. We also find in Samuel's yearly circuit as judge Gilgal received a regular visits. Not again until Elijah's day do we find information about sons of the prophets at Gilgal. 2 Kings 2:1" And it came to pass, when the LORD would take up Elijah into heaven by a whirlwind, that Elijah went with Elisha from Gilgal." The two prophets were probably giving instruction at The School of the Prophets at Gilgal. On their way they stop at two other schools to leave a parting word. 2 Kings 2:3-5 *"And the sons of the prophets that were at Bethel came forth to Elisha, and said unto him, Knowest thou that the LORD will take away thy master from thy head to day? And he said, Yea, I know it; hold ye your peace. And Elijah said unto him, Elisha, tarry here, I pray thee; for the LORD hath sent me to Jericho. And he said, As the LORD liveth, and as thy soul liveth, I will not leave thee. So they came to Jericho. And the sons of the prophets that were at Jericho came to Elisha, and said unto him, Knowest thou that the LORD will take away thy master from thy head to day? And he answered, Yea, I know it; hold ye your peace."* Several years later there was a famine in the land and while Elisha was visiting the School of the Prophets at Gilgal he performed miracles. During this time period we learn that there were about one hundred of these sons of the prophets in Gilgal. 2 Kings 4:38,43 *"And Elisha came again to Gilgal: and there was a dearth in the land; and the sons of the prophets were sitting before him: and he said unto his servant, Set on the great pot, and seethe pottage for the sons of the prophets. 43 And his servitor said, What, should I set this before an hundred men? He said again, Give the people, that they may eat: for thus saith the LORD, They shall eat, and shall leave thereof."*

Jericho

The third stopping place of Elijah and Elisha on their way to Elijah's translation was at Jericho. Here Elijah gives his last exhortation to the sons of the prophets. After this was done they went on to the Jordan. 2 Kings 2:4-7 *"And Elijah said unto him, Elisha, tarry here, I pray thee; for the LORD hath sent me to Jericho. And he said, As the LORD liveth, and as thy soul liveth, I will not leave thee. So they came to Jericho. And the sons of the prophets that were at Jericho came to Elisha, and said unto him,*

Knowest thou that the LORD will take away thy master from thy head to day? And he answered, Yea, I know it; hold ye your peace. And Elijah said unto him, Tarry, I pray thee, here; for the LORD hath sent me to Jordan. And he said, As the LORD liveth, and as thy soul liveth, I will not leave thee. And they two went on. And fifty men of the sons of the prophets went, and stood to view afar off: and they two stood by Jordan." After the translation of Elijah, Elisha returns to Jericho and tarries three days with the sons of the prophets. The Word of God also tells us that there building got too small and they had to build a bigger one. 2 Kings 6:1-2 *"And the sons of the prophets said unto Elisha, Behold now, the place where we dwell with thee is too strait for us. Let us go, we pray thee, unto Jordan, and take thence every man a beam, and let us make us a place there, where we may dwell. And he answered, Go ye."*

Mount Carmel

We find Elisa visiting Mount Carmel after visiting other cities with known Schools of the Prophets. In 1 Kings 2 we find that Elisha on his return from the Jordan and Jericho went to Bethel and from there to Mount Carmel. When the Shunammite woman was grieving over the death of her son she went unto Elisha at Mount Carmel. 2 Kings 4:25 *"So she went and came unto the man of God to mount Carmel. And it came to pass, when the man of God saw her afar off, that he said to Gehazi his servant, Behold, yonder is that Shunammite."* This must have been a place he was at on a regular basis, because it was neither newmoon nor sabbath, at which times he undoubtedly held special services at places other than the schools. Mount Carmel may have been chosen as a school for the sons of the prophets in recognition of the test between Elijah and the false prophets.

Samaria

Samuel had his greatest school in his home town of Ramah so it is logical that Elisha would have a school at his home town of Samaria. 2 Kings 5:3 *"And she said unto her mistress, Would God my lord were with the prophet that is in Samaria! for he would recover him of his leprosy."* We see evidence of sons of the prophets at Bethel and Mount Carmel and here is a recorded journey to these cities with a return to Samaria. 2 Kings 2:23-25 *"And he went up from thence unto Bethel: and as he was going up by the way, there came forth little children out of the city, and mocked him, and said unto him, Go up, thou bald head; go up, thou bald head. And he turned back, and looked on them, and cursed them in the name of the LORD. And there came forth two she bears out of the wood, and tare forty and two children of them. And he went from thence to mount Carmel, and from thence he returned to Samaria."* At Bethel and probably at Mount Carmel, Elisha had already visited the Schools of the Prophets. We find during the persecutions of Jezebel, Obadiah took an hundred prophets and hid them by fifty in a cave, and fed them with bread and water. 1 Kings 18:2-4 *"And Elijah went to shew himself unto Ahab. And there was a sore famine in Samaria. And Ahab called Obadiah, which was the governor of his house. (Now Obadiah feared the LORD greatly: For it was so, when Jezebel cut off the prophets of the LORD, that Obadiah took an hundred prophets, and hid them by fifty in a cave, and fed them with bread and water.)"* Also when Jehoshaphat and Ahab were about to go to war with Ramoth Gilead they gathered the prophets together. 1 Kings 22:6 *"Then the king of Israel gathered the prophets together, about four hundred men, and said unto them, Shall I go against Ramothgilead to battle, or shall I forbear? And they said, Go up; for the Lord shall deliver it into the hand of the king."* This passage reveals that at Samaria there was a large numbers of prophets.

We Need Teaching Today

The Apostle Paul setup in a school while he was at Ephesus and taught his disciples.   Acts 19:9-10 *"But when divers were hardened, and believed not, but spake evil of that way before the multitude, he departed from them, and separated the disciples, disputing daily in the school of one Tyrannus. And this continued by the space of two years; so that all they which dwelt in Asia heard the word of the Lord Jesus, both Jews and Greeks."* One of the fivefold ministry positions is a teacher. We must have teaching if we are going to grow in our faith and love. Ephesians 4:11-16 *"And he gave some, apostles; and some, prophets; and some, evangelists; and some, pastors and teachers; For the perfecting of the saints, for the work of the ministry, for the edifying of the body of Christ: Till we all come in the unity of the faith, and of the knowledge of the Son of God, unto a perfect man, unto the measure of the stature of the fulness of Christ: That we henceforth be no more children, tossed to and fro, and carried about with every wind of doctrine, by the sleight of men, and cunning craftiness, whereby they lie in wait to deceive; But speaking the truth in love, may grow up into him in all things, which is the head, even Christ: From whom the whole body fitly joined together and compacted by that which every joint supplieth, according to the effectual working in the measure of every part, maketh increase of the body unto the edifying of itself in love."* If you are not actively studying the Word of God you are going to be weak and anemic. We need to fall in love with the Word of God and look at it as our daily spiritual bread from heaven. To love God is too want to get to know everything about God that is possible. It is only by hearing the Word of God that we are going to build our faith.   Romans 10:17 *"So then faith cometh by hearing, and hearing by the word of God."* By learning the Word of God to the point that it is hidden in our heart we are able to defeat sin and become victorious in faith. Psalms 119:10-12 *"With my whole heart have I sought thee: O let me not wander from thy commandments. Thy word have I hid in mine heart, that I might not sin against thee. Blessed art thou, O LORD: teach me thy statutes."* So many stumble and fall in their walk with God because they do not know about the blessings He has for them. In order to take advantage of all the power and glory of the Kingdom of God, we must learn of His holy ways.

We need more than just a surface knowledge of the Word of God. Oh, that we would yearn for the deep things of God. 1 Corinthians 2:6-14 *"Howbeit we speak wisdom among them that are perfect: yet not the wisdom of this world, nor of the princes of this world, that come to nought: But we speak the wisdom of God in a mystery, even the hidden wisdom, which God ordained before the world unto our glory: Which none of the princes of this world knew: for had they known it, they would not have crucified the Lord of glory. But as it is written, Eye hath not seen, nor ear heard, neither have entered into the heart of man, the things which God hath prepared for them that love him. But God hath revealed them unto us by his Spirit: for the Spirit searcheth all things, yea, the deep things of God. For what man knoweth the things of a man, save the spirit of man which is in him? even so the things of God knoweth no man, but the Spirit of God. Now we have received, not the spirit of the world, but the spirit which is of God; that we might know the things that are freely given to us of God. Which things also we speak, not in the words which man's wisdom teacheth, but which the Holy Ghost teacheth; comparing spiritual things with spiritual. But the natural man receiveth not the things of the Spirit of God: for they are foolishness unto him: neither can he know them, because they are spiritually discerned."* When we learn of the deep things of God we become a powerhouse of faith and truth ready to take the strongholds of Satan and set the captives free.

The Word of God is a gold mine, just waiting for you to mine out the nuggets and truth. What riches and glory awaits those who take possession of the truth and refuse to sell it at any price. We cannot be full of the world and be able to receive the gold of the Kingdom. You must first unload the filth of this world before you can load up on the golden blessings of the Lord. Revelation 3:15-22 *"I know thy works, that thou art neither cold nor hot: I would thou wert cold or hot. So then because thou art lukewarm, and neither cold nor hot, I will spue thee out of my mouth. Because thou sayest, I am rich, and increased with goods, and have need of nothing; and knowest not that thou art wretched, and miserable, and poor, and blind, and naked: I counsel thee to buy of me gold tried in the fire, that thou mayest be rich; and white raiment, that thou mayest be clothed, and that the shame of thy nakedness do not appear; and anoint thine eyes with eyesalve, that thou mayest see. As many as I love, I rebuke and chasten: be zealous therefore, and repent. Behold, I stand at the door, and knock: if any man hear my voice, and open the door, I will come in to him, and will sup with him, and he with me. To him that overcometh will I grant to sit with me in my throne, even as I also overcame, and am set down with my Father in his throne. He that hath an ear, let him hear what the Spirit saith unto the churches."* We have before us an open door and Jesus is on the other side knocking. It is time to open that door and learn of the riches of the Kingdom.

It is not a journey for the lazy or faint of heart. It will take hard work and study. There will be things in your life you must lay aside in order to train for victory. You have what it takes to become a champion if you will pay the price. The blessings of the

Kingdom are worth more than anything the world can offer. Proverbs 23:23 *"Buy the truth, and sell it not; also wisdom, and instruction, and understanding."* The miraculous will only come when we are equipped with the instruction of faith. 2 Timothy 2:2-7 *"And the things that thou hast heard of me among many witnesses, the same commit thou to faithful men, who shall be able to teach others also. Thou therefore endure hardness, as a good soldier of Jesus Christ. No man that warreth entangleth himself with the affairs of this life; that he may please him who hath chosen him to be a soldier. And if a man also strive for masteries, yet is he not crowned, except he strive lawfully. The husbandman that laboureth must be first partaker of the fruits. Consider what I say; and the Lord give thee understanding in all things."* 2 Timothy 2:15 *"Study to shew thyself approved unto God, a workman that needeth not to be ashamed, rightly dividing the word of truth."* Let us open our Bibles and begin to study like our life depends on it, because it does.

Discussion Questions

1. Who were the leaders of the sons of the prophets?

____

____

____

2. What gifts has God set in the church?

____

____

____

3. Where was the home of Elisha?

____

____

____

4. What happen to the seventy elders of Moses before they prophesied?

____

____

____

5. What did Obadiah do for the prophets in Samaria?

____

____

____

DOUBLE PORTION
The Miracles Of Elisha

Lesson Two

Parting Of The Waters

God wants to use you to work miracles in your world. The first time can be a very intimidating experience, but it does not have to be if you have good teachers. Today we are going to study about the first miracle in the life of the prophet Elisha. God is faithful and will work in your life just like he has worked in the lives of those who have blazed a trail before us today. Be faithful to your man of God and you will see the power of God begin to be demonstrated in your life too. Let us study about the miracles from the Word of God so we will be ready to let the Lord use us when the time comes.

Scripture Text

2 Kings 2:1-18 "*And it came to pass, when the LORD would take up Elijah into heaven by a whirlwind, that Elijah went with Elisha from Gilgal. 2 And Elijah said unto Elisha, Tarry here, I pray thee; for the LORD hath sent me to Bethel. And Elisha said unto him, As the LORD liveth, and as thy soul liveth, I will not leave thee. So they went down to Bethel. 3 And the sons of the prophets that were at Bethel came forth to Elisha, and said unto him, Knowest*

thou that the LORD will take away thy master from thy head to day? And he said, Yea, I know it; hold ye your peace. 4 And Elijah said unto him, Elisha, tarry here, I pray thee; for the LORD hath sent me to Jericho. And he said, As the LORD liveth, and as thy soul liveth, I will not leave thee. So they came to Jericho. 5 And the sons of the prophets that were at Jericho came to Elisha, and said unto him, Knowest thou that the LORD will take away thy master from thy head to day? And he answered, Yea, I know it; hold ye your peace. 6 And Elijah said unto him, Tarry, I pray thee, here; for the LORD hath sent me to Jordan. And he said, As the LORD liveth, and as thy soul liveth, I will not leave thee. And they two went on. 7 And fifty men of the sons of the prophets went, and stood to view afar off: and they two stood by Jordan. 8 And Elijah took his mantle, and wrapped it together, and smote the waters, and they were divided hither and thither, so that they two went over on dry ground. 9 And it came to pass, when they were gone over, that Elijah said unto Elisha, Ask what I shall do for thee, before I be taken away from thee. And Elisha said, I pray thee, let a double portion of thy spirit be upon me. 10 And he said, Thou hast asked a hard thing: nevertheless, if thou see me when I am taken from thee, it shall be so unto thee; but if not, it shall not be so. 11 And it came to pass, as they still went on, and talked, that, behold, there appeared a chariot of fire, and horses of fire, and parted them both asunder; and Elijah went up by a whirlwind into heaven. 12 And Elisha saw it, and he cried, My father, my father, the chariot of Israel, and the horsemen thereof. And he saw him no more: and he took hold of his own clothes, and rent them in two pieces. 13 He took up also the mantle of Elijah that fell from him, and went back, and stood by the bank of Jordan; 14 And he took the mantle of Elijah that fell from him, and smote the waters, and said, Where is the LORD God of Elijah? and when he also had smitten the waters, they parted hither and thither: and Elisha went over. 15 And when the sons of the prophets which were to view at Jericho saw him, they said, The spirit of Elijah doth rest on Elisha. And they came to meet him, and bowed themselves to the ground before him. 16 And they said unto him, Behold now, there be with thy servants fifty strong men; let them go, we pray thee, and seek thy master: lest peradventure the Spirit of the LORD hath taken him up, and cast him upon some mountain, or into some valley. And he said, Ye shall not send. 17 And when they urged him till he was ashamed, he said, Send. They sent therefore fifty men; and they sought three days, but found him not. 18 And when they came again to *him, (for he tarried at Jericho,) he said unto them, Did I not say unto you, Go not?"*

The Last Journey

2 Kings 2:1 *"And it came to pass, when the LORD would take up Elijah into heaven by a whirlwind, that Elijah went with Elisha from Gilgal."*

God had determined to take Elijah up into heaven by a whirlwind. God probably let him know of his plan some time before, that He would shortly take him from the world, not by death, but translate him body and soul to heaven as he had done to Enoch. It is not for us to say why God would put such a special honor upon Elijah above the other prophets. He was a man subject to like passions as we are, knew sin and yet never tasted death. Wherefore is he thus distinguished as a man whom the King of Kings did delight to honor. God looked back upon his past service, which was faithful and dedicated. This was to reward him for his service and also to encourage the sons of the prophets to tread in the steps of his passion and faithfulness. God wanted the sons of the prophets to be motivated to preach against the corruptions of the age they lived in, regardless of the cost. God looked forward to the church age and in the translation of Elijah, gave a type and shadow of the ascension of Christ and the opening of the Kingdom of God to all believers. Elijah had proven his relationship with God by faith and prayer and now he is taken to heaven to assure us that if we are born again while we are here on earth, we shall be in heaven shortly, the soul shall be happy there forever more.

Faithful And Loyal

2 Kings 2-2 *"And Elijah said unto Elisha, Tarry here, I pray thee; for the LORD hath sent me to Bethel. And Elisha said unto him, As the LORD liveth, and as thy soul liveth, I will not leave thee. So they went down to Bethel."*

Elisha had determined, as long as Elijah continued on earth he was going to cleave to him and not to leave him. Elijah seemed desirous to shake him off, would have had him stay behind at Gilgal, at Bethel and at Jericho (2 Kings 2:2,4,6). Elisha was tested three time to see if he would be faithful. He was tested at Gilgal, the site of the first camp of the Israelite in the promise land

and first covenant (Joshua 5:8). You will have to pass the test of obedience to Acts 2:38 and the New Testament church doctrine when you first come to God. He was tested at Bethel, which was the place that Jacob (Israel) named the "The House of God." You will have to pass the test of being faithful to the house of God. He was tested at Jericho, which was the first fruits or tithes and was given to God when conquered. You will have to pass the test of being faithful in paying of tithes and giving of offerings. Without passing these three test and being faithful to your Pastor there will never be a mantle of anointing handed down to you.

Elijah knew what honor God designed for him but did not want to flaunt it, nor desired that it should be seen of men. God's faithful do not want to have their miracles proclaimed as a great work they have done, but the carnal ministers of denominal religions do. But real men of God always wants God to get the glory. Perhaps it was to try Elisha and make his following of Elijah the more meaningful, like Naomi trying to persuading Ruth to go back. In vain does Elijah ask him to stay here and stay there; he resolves to stay nowhere but with his master till he goes to heaven and leaves him behind on this earth. *"Whatever comes of it, I will not leave thee."* Not only did he love him but he desired to be edified by his fellowship and instruction as long as he stayed on earth; it had always been a blessing to him. We may assume the fellowship was a blessing now more than ever. We should do all we can to bless one another. We should glean as much as we can from the elders while we are together, because they have so much to give and we have so little time left to receive it. When God takes his faithful ones to heaven, death is the Jordan which they must pass through. The death of Christ has made a way for the redeemed to pass over with peace. 1 Corinthians 15:55-57 *"O death, where is thy sting? O grave, where is thy victory? The sting of death is sin; and the strength of sin is the law. But thanks be to God, which giveth us the victory through our Lord Jesus Christ."* Elisha desired to be sure of Elijah departure and to see him when he was taken up that his faith might be strengthen. He had long followed Elijah and he would not leave him now when he hoped for a parting blessing. Let not those that follow Jesus come up short by becoming weary in well doing.

The Final Goodbye

2 Kings 2-3 *"And the sons of the prophets that were at*

Bethel came forth to Elisha, and said unto him, Knowest thou that the LORD will take away thy master from thy head to day? And he said, Yea, I know it; hold ye your peace."

Elijah visited The Schools of the Prophets before his departure and told them goodbye. There were schools of the prophets in several of the cities in Israel. Here we find sons of the prophets and a considerable numbers of them. They were at Bethel where one of the calves was set up and at Jericho which was lately rebuilt in defiance of a divine curse. God had ordained those schools to train men in the exercises of prophesy and worship and thereby righteousness was preached in a time of general apostasy. None of the high priests were comparable to those two great prophets Elijah and Elisha, which had no record of ever attending in the temple at Jerusalem. Elijah now visits The Schools of the Prophets before his departure, to instruct, encourage and bless them. Those that could soon go to heaven ought to be concerned for those they leave behind them on earth. They should leave with them their experiences, testimonies, counsels and prayers. All of the elders need to find someone and pour themselves into them. All of the young men and women need to be looking for someone to fill them with their wisdom and anointing. Listen before it is too late.

Told Again

2 Kings 2-4:6 *"And Elijah said unto him, Elisha, tarry here, I pray thee; for the LORD hath sent me to Jericho. And he said, As the LORD liveth, and as thy soul liveth, I will not leave thee. So they came to Jericho. And the sons of the prophets that were at Jericho came to Elisha, and said unto him, Knowest thou that the LORD will take away thy master from thy head to day? And he answered, Yea, I know it; hold ye your peace. And Elijah said unto him, Tarry, I pray thee, here; for the LORD hath sent me to Jordan. And he said, As the LORD liveth, and as thy soul liveth, I will not leave thee. And they two went on."*

The sons of the prophets had been informed either by Elijah himself, or by the spirit of prophecy by someone of their own school, or suspected by Elijah's farewell, that he was shortly to be with them no more. They told Elisha of it, both at Bethel (2 Kings 2:3) and at Jericho (2 Kings 2:5.)   They said this to help Elisha prepare for the loss. We never know when one our nearest relations or dearest friends may be taken from us. We all have an appointment with death, so let us be ready at all times to meet the Lord. He takes away elders from our head, saints from our arms and family from our household. Let us live peaceful with all men so that we may reflect upon the past with comfort when it comes time to part. Elisha knew the time was at hand and sorrow had filled his heart (as the disciples did in John 16:6) and therefore he did not want to be told of it, did not care to hear it again and would not be interrupted in his giving of full attention to the end or diverted from his following of his master. "I know it, hold you your peace" he tells them. He speaks not with anger to the sons of the prophets but as one that was respectful and would have them to be respectful also. It was time to be silent and prepare for what was to come. As they left, fifty of them stood to watch at a distance. They wanted to satisfy their curiosity, but God's plan was for them not to be eye witnesses of the honor God gave to His prophet who was rejected and despised of men. We should pay attention to God's works, because when God opens a door, He always has a plan. It is always a journey of greater blessing to help us go up higher.

His Last Miracle

> 2 Kings 2:7-8 *"And fifty men of the sons of the prophets went, and stood to view afar off: and they two stood by Jordan. And Elijah took his mantle, and wrapped it together, and smote the waters, and they were divided hither and thither, so that they two went over on dry ground."*

The miraculous dividing of the river Jordan was the precursor to Elijah's translation into heaven, as it had been to the entrance of Israel into the earthly Canaan. The Lord was taking him to the other side Jordan to be translated. It was his home land and it was near the place where Moses died. Elijah and Elisha might have gone over Jordan by a ferry, as other passengers did, but God would confirm Elijah in his exit, as he did Joshua in his entrance, by the dividing of this river (Joshua 3:7). As Moses with his rod divided the sea, so Elijah with his mantle divided Jordan, both being the symbols of God working in their ministry. These waters of old yielded to the Ark of the Covenant, now to the prophet's mantle. The Ark of the Covenant represented God's presence. The mantle represented God's anointing.

It Is Finished

> 2 Kings 2:9-12 *" And it came to pass, when they were gone over, that Elijah said unto Elisha, Ask what I shall do for thee, before I be taken away from thee. And Elisha said, I pray thee, let a double portion of thy spirit be upon me. And he said, Thou hast asked a hard thing: nevertheless, if thou see me when I am taken from thee, it shall be so unto thee; but if not, it shall not be so. And it came to pass, as they still went on, and talked, that, behold, there appeared a chariot of fire, and horses of fire, and parted them both asunder; and Elijah went up by a whirlwind into heaven. And Elisha saw it, and he cried, My father, my father, the chariot of Israel, and the horsemen thereof. And he saw him no more: and he took hold of his own clothes, and rent them in two pieces.*

The asking for the double portion showed Elisha great respect for the power that the Lord had anointed Elijah with. Some try to make this asking for a double portion like the inheritance of the first born son. Deuteronomy 21:17 *"But he shall acknowledge the son of the hated for the firstborn, by giving him a double portion of all that he hath: for he is the beginning of his strength; the right of the firstborn is his."* But Elisha was not looking for carnal possessions. He was hungry for the Spirit of the Lord to be upon him. We see the Spirit of Lord that was upon Moses passed on to the leaders who were anointed to rule under him. Numbers 11:16 -17 *"And the LORD said unto Moses, Gather unto me seventy men of the elders of Israel, whom thou knowest to be the elders of the people, and officers over them; and bring them unto the tabernacle of the congregation, that they may stand there with thee. And I will come down and talk with thee there: and I will take of the spirit which is upon thee, and will put it upon them; and they shall bear the burden of the people with thee, that thou bear it not thyself alone."* We are blessed that because of Calvary, each and every one of us can be filled with the God's Spirit today. During the Old Testament we see the Spirit of God coming mainly upon His prophets and not the common man. But even today there is a special anointing and gift that comes upon the ministry when they are anointed and prayed over by the presbytery. 1 Timothy 4:14 *"Neglect not the gift that is in thee, which was given thee by prophecy, with the laying on of the hands of the presbytery."* If we want to be mightily used of God today, we need to have the mantle of anointing passed on to us by our pastor. It is also obvious that Elijah was attributed with seven great miracles whereas Elisha was attributed with fourteen great miracles. That is double the amount of great miracles that Elisha was used to perform. All that some can see is the miracles and fail to see the great responsibility that now rested upon the shoulders of Elisha to lead the nation of Israel. There are many who can fight but they cannot govern. It is just as great a victory to be able to have a united church as to build a new church. What have we accomplished if our fruit does not remain? John 15:16 *"Ye have not chosen me, but I have chosen you, and ordained you, that ye should go and bring forth fruit, and that your fruit should remain: that whatsoever ye shall ask of the Father in my name, he may give it you."*

Taking Up The Mantle

> 2 Kings 2:13-14 *"He took up also the mantle of Elijah that fell from him, and went back, and stood by the bank of Jordan; And he took the mantle of Elijah that fell from him, and smote the waters, and said, Where is the LORD God of Elijah? and when he also had smitten the waters, they parted hither and thither: and Elisha went over."*

Elisha suddenly finds himself on his own. How short the gap between the two prophets and how easily filled it is! Not even the greatest are indispensable. God lays aside one tool, but only to take up another. He will use any willing vessel. The work goes on, though the workers change and there is little time for self-pity and none for idle sorrow. Elisha's first miracle is used to prove to him and the sons of the prophets that God has given him a double portion. The mantle which lay at his feet had been thrown to him by Elijah when he was called to his reward and it was now a token that the office and power had transferred to him. The transference of the mantle of anointing was a pledge to him that he had been appointed successor. It was an outward token to others that the Spirit that was upon Elijah, was now resting upon him. He begins by closely walking in the tracks of Elijah, a wise and humble man, called to do a work for God. The repetition of the miracle of the parting of the Jordan by the same means and the calling on the Lord as the "God of Elijah" shows the transfer of anointing. The God of Elijah is now given the same importance as the terms; the God of Abraham and Isaac and Jacob. His prayer was framed like a question and shows that Elisha did not have full confidence in his relationship with God because he had not proven his relationship with God yet. "Where is the Lord God of Elijah?" is not the question of unbelief, but neither is it the voice of full confidence.   A voice of confidence and experience would ask no such question, because it knows Him to be with you. It is the cry that expresses, Oh that Thou mayest be here, even with unworthy me! The faith was real, though young and clouded with some uncertainty. Remember that all of us will have trails of our faith.   His fervent prayer of a righteous man was answered because Elisha trusted in God.   The waters parted and all of Elisha's doubt was washed away.   God will listen to men who plead for past miracles to be repeated today. By Him answering the cry addressed to Him as the God of the Elders of old, it will embolden us to cry to Him later as our very own God.   He is still a God who answers prayers by miracles. We can be dependent on His promises.

The Responsibility Of Leadership

> 2 Kings 2:15 *"And when the sons of the prophets which were to view at Jericho saw him, they said, The spirit of Elijah doth rest on Elisha. And they came to meet him, and bowed themselves to the ground before him."*

The miracle was worked partly for Elisha and partly for others who were to acknowledge his authority. The striking of the mantle on the river and the miraculous division of the waters because of it was evidence that the Lord God of Elijah was with him.   This miracle was witnessed by the sons of the prophets from Jericho, they now recognized the ordination of Elisha as the prophet of Israel. These sons of the prophets who stood on the eastern bank of Jordan had not witnessed the translation. But they saw Elisha returning alone and the waters parting before him and no doubt as he came nearer they recognized what he bore in his hand, Elijah's well-known mantle. They hasten to recognize him as the head of the prophets. Their acknowledgment of Elisha as the ordained prophet of God places him in a place to lead them. Elijah's spirit rests on him and now he must lead the people. Elisha ministry was different than Elijah. He was not one to start new works or bring new revelations. He carries on what Elijah had begun. He inherits a work and is what Timothy was to Paul, a son in the faith. The same Spirit was on him but his personality and works were different than his underdog predecessor. Elisha had no such battles as Elijah. He did not engage in a one on one battle with murderous kings and queens. He did not engage in a single handed effort to stop a whole nation from forsaking God. He had no fiery energy or bursts of despair. Elisha worked with kings as an honored guest and trusted counsellor. He did not dwell apart like Elijah did at times in the desert but lived in the fertile valley of the Jordan. He lived a life at peace among his brethren and was loved and respected by many. His miracles are mostly works of mercy and gentleness. He provided for the needs and healed sicknesses. His works dried tears and gave back dear ones to mourners. He was a complete contrast to his stern, solitary, forceful predecessor. It is like the difference of a still small voice to the roar of the winds of the storm. There are diversities of operations, but the same God. It is well to remember that God's blessings on our brothers does not exhaust the possibilities of God's goodness upon us. God will always bless us according to our needs. We all must join hands in serving the same Lord in diverse ways, which are all needed. We should seek to understand and discern the many gifts of the Spirit which operates in the church. Elijah and Elisha or Paul and Timothy were both His servants which worked in different fields of labor. It is time for the strong to recognize the power of the gentle and the gentle to discern the love of the strong. Let us work together to keep the unity of the faith. Let us realize that our brother does a work for the Lord the same as we do.

The Gentle Prophet

> 2 Kings 2:16-18 *"And they said unto him, Behold now, there be with thy servants fifty strong men; let them go, we pray thee, and seek thy master: lest peradventure the Spirit of the LORD hath taken him up, and cast him upon some mountain, or into some valley. And he said, Ye shall not send. And when they urged him till he was ashamed, he said, Send. They sent therefore fifty men; and they sought three days, but found him not. And when they came again to him, (for he tarried at Jericho,) he said unto them, Did I not say unto you, Go not?"*

The search for Elijah insisted on by the sons of the prophets is of importance only as a way of showing their carnality and Elisha's gentle spirit. He is their leader but he rules with meekness. Can you imagine anybody urging Elijah till he was ashamed? No doubt Elisha had told them what had happened but the sons of the prophet think that Elijah has been miraculously whisked away as he had been before and was just somewhere else on the earth. They have no notion of what had really happened. How hard it is to get carnal men to understand the things of the Spirit! I can hear the sons of the prophets proclaim "Surely he is not gone up to heaven. He is lying, living or dead, in some valley or on some mountain. Let us go and look for him!" There are many who are blind to God's way of doing things. To go looking for a man who had been taken to heaven was carnal thinking.   But Elisha's gentleness is to be noted. He let them try it their way. Often that is the only way of convincing carnal people of their errors. When the fifty sons of the prophets come back empty handed, all he says is a quiet "Did I not say unto you, Go not?" 2 Timothy 2:23-26 *"But foolish and unlearned questions avoid, knowing that they do gender strifes. And the servant of the Lord must not strive; but be gentle unto all men, apt to teach, patient, In meekness instructing those that oppose themselves; if God peradventure will give them repentance to the acknowledging of the truth; And that they may recover themselves out of the snare of the devil, who are taken captive by him at his will."*

Discussion Questions

1. Why was it important for Elisha not to leave Elijah?

____

____

____

2. Who and where did they visit on their journey?

____

____

____

3. What was Timothy given by the laying on of the hands of the presbytery?

____

____

____

4. What did the mantle represent to Elisha?

____

____

____

5. How did Elisha rule the sons of the prophets?

____

____

____

DOUBLE PORTION
The Miracles Of Elisha

Lesson Three

God Is Not Mocked

Not all miracles make logical sense and not all miracles leave the recipient with a warm fuzzy feeling. The sword of the Lord is double edged, one side is a side of blessings and the other side brings a curse. We see this demonstrated in our lesson today. A miracle of restoration is worked in Jericho and a curse is placed and a miracle comes about because of it in Bethel. We will be encouraged today because we will see the restoration power of God demonstrated. Also we will be sadden to see the sins of the parents passed down to their children. It is always a hard thing to stand by and see the judgements of God poured out upon the wicked. But mankind will never get around the law of harvest. Galatians 6:7-8 *"Be not deceived; God is not mocked: for whatsoever a man soweth, that shall he also reap. For he that soweth to his flesh shall of the flesh reap corruption; but he that soweth to the Spirit shall of the Spirit reap life everlasting."* Many times these displays of judgement on earth are done by God to provide grace to the recipient. God is trying to show mankind he is sewing the wrong crop. When the crop comes to harvest and provides its bitter fruit in the life of the wicked they are given a wakeup call and an opportunity to repent before it is too late. God tolerating mankind doing as he pleases is not the grace of God. The grace of God is not a credit card given to mankind with no limits and never a payday. The grace of God will not allow mankind to sin forever and still have salvation. Many times this grace of God is displayed in the life of mankind as a judgement. Titus 2:11-14 *"For the grace of God that bringeth salvation hath appeared to all men, Teaching us that, denying ungodliness and worldly lusts, we should live soberly, righteously, and Godly, in this present world; Looking for that blessed hope, and the glorious appearing of the great God and our Saviour Jesus Christ; Who gave himself for us, that he might redeem us from all iniquity, and purify unto himself a peculiar people, zealous of good works."* Sin sometimes provides pleasure for a season. But many times the sinner then spends the rest of their life reaping the bitter fruits of pain and suffering. Hebrews 11:24-26 *"By faith Moses, when he was come to years, refused to be called the son of Pharaoh's daughter; Choosing rather to suffer affliction with the people of God, than to enjoy the pleasures of sin for a season; Esteeming the reproach of Christ greater riches than the treasures in Egypt: for he had respect unto the recompence of the reward."*

Scripture Text

2 Kings 2:19-25 *"And the men of the city said unto Elisha, Behold, I pray thee, the situation of this city is pleasant, as my lord seeth: but the water is naught, and the ground barren. 20 And he said, Bring me a new cruse, and put salt therein. And they brought it to him. 21 And he went forth unto the spring of the waters, and cast the salt in there, and said, Thus saith the LORD, I have healed these waters; there shall not be from thence any more death or barren land. 22 So the waters were healed unto this day, according to the saying of Elisha which he spake. 23 And he went up from thence unto Bethel: and as he was going up by the*

way, there came forth little children out of the city, and mocked him, and said unto him, Go up, thou bald head; go up, thou bald head. 24 And he turned back, and looked on them, and cursed them in the name of the LORD. And there came forth two she bears out of the wood, and tare forty and two children of them. 25 And he went from thence to mount Carmel, and from thence he returned to Samaria."

What Is A Biblical Curse?

There are many instances of curses in the Bible. The word "curse" is often used in contrast to the word "blessings". God cursed the serpent that had seduced Eve (Genesis 3:14) and Cain who slew his brother (Genesis 4:11), both of these were judgements pronounced upon wrongdoing. Curses given by the man of God are not an expression of revenge, power or impatience, they are predictions of forthcoming judgement. A curse is not the use of magic spells which enlists the support of a higher power to persuade them to carry out the suppliant's wishes. A curse is always the judgement of God against those who have sinned against Him. Ecclesiastes 8:11-13 *"Because sentence against an evil work is not executed speedily, therefore the heart of the sons of men is fully set in them to do evil. Though a sinner do evil an hundred times, and his days be prolonged, yet surely I know that it shall be well with them that fear God, which fear before him: But it shall not be well with the wicked, neither shall he prolong his days, which are as a shadow; because he feareth not before God."* The judgements of God are designed to help mankind have a fear of God. God does not run on the same time table that we run on but His word does come to pass. The fear of God will help motivate us to do right. When we do right we will be blessed and find joy. When we do evil we will be cursed and live in misery. Many times the Word of God tells us the consequences of sin, which we will see plainly demonstrated in our lesson today. We will also see that when man repents and does right that the judgement (curse) can end and blessings can begin to flow.

Remember, there is hope for the mockers. They will have the judgement of God poured out upon them but if they repent and fear God they can be pulled out of the fire. Jude 1:17-23 *"But, beloved, remember ye the words which were spoken before of the apostles of our Lord Jesus Christ; How that they told you there should be mockers in the last time, who should walk after their own ungodly lusts. These be they who separate themselves, sensual, having not the Spirit. But ye, beloved, building up yourselves on your most holy faith, praying in the Holy Ghost, Keep yourselves in the love of God, looking for the mercy of our Lord Jesus Christ unto eternal life. And of some have compassion, making a difference: And others save with fear, pulling them out of the fire; hating even the garment spotted by the flesh."* The church today needs to remember that the sword of the Lord has two sides. One side of the sword brings blessings. The other side of the sword brings a curse (judgement).

The Miracle At Jericho

> 2 Kings 2:19-22 *"And the men of the city said unto Elisha, Behold, I pray thee, the situation of this city is pleasant, as my lord seeth: but the water is naught, and the ground barren. 20 And he said, Bring me a new cruse, and put salt therein. And they brought it to him. 21 And he went forth unto the spring of the waters, and cast the salt in there, and said, Thus saith the LORD, I have healed these waters; there shall not be from thence any more death or barren land. 22 So the waters were healed unto this day, according to the saying of Elisha which he spake."*

We find the first city conquered after the children of Israel come out of Egypt was Jericho. The inhabitants of Jericho was the Canaanites. Because of the mockery of Ham, all of his decedents (Canaanites) were cursed. Genesis 9:25 *"And he said, Cursed be Canaan; a servant of servants shall he be unto his brethren."* Jericho was the first fruits of conquest and God required all the spoils of Jericho be given to him as the tithes. This is why God made a big deal out of Achan taking the wedge of gold and Babylonian garment. He was robbing God by not paying his tithes. Then Joshua curses Jericho. Joshua 6:26 *"And Joshua adjured them at that time, saying, Cursed be the man before the LORD, that riseth up and buildeth this city Jericho: he shall lay the foundation thereof in his firstborn, and in his youngest son shall he set up the gates of it."* Let us notice that the city where so many received the judgements of God was the same city where Rahab the harlot was blessed with salvation because she believed and obeyed the men of God. We cannot blame our circumstances when we make bad decisions. God will give us the opportunity to be blessed when everything around us is being cursed.

During the time of Elisha, Jericho had been rebuilt in spite of the curse against its builders and it was costing dearly. 1 Kings 16:34 *"In his days did Hiel the Bethelite build Jericho: he laid the foundation thereof in Abiram his firstborn, and set up the gates thereof in his youngest son Segub, according to the word of the LORD, which he spake by Joshua the son of Nun."* The poison spewing forth out of the spring seems to have been part of the curse. It appears that the water did not turn naught until after the city was rebuilt. For men would not be so foolish as to rebuild a city which had only bad water to depend on. So we see that sin is a gift that keeps on giving if it is not repented of. Numbers 14:18 *"The LORD is longsuffering, and of great mercy, forgiving iniquity and transgression, and by no means clearing the guilty, visiting the iniquity of the fathers upon the children unto the third and fourth generation."* History tells us that the water caused the cattle to abort their babies, the plants to drop their fruit before it was ripe, and even the women to be incapable of childbirth.

We all know that adding salt to water makes it undrinkable and destructive to crops. So to the carnal mind the adding of salt to the water would not heal it. Romans 8:6-7 *"For to be carnally minded is death; but to be spiritually minded is life and peace. Because the carnal mind is enmity against God: for it is not subject to the law of God, neither indeed can be.*" We may not understand how the commandments of God are necessary but everything God commands has a purpose. God is always looking for us to react to His words before He brings the blessings. That is why it is important for us to pray after we have heard the preaching of the Word of God. When God speaks to us, He wants a response. To leave the House of God indifferent will not bring the blessings. We need to commit to the promises of God. If they had not done their part and added the salt to the water it would have never been healed. The salt is also symbolic of what God wants us to be today. After Jesus got done giving us the beatitudes or the prescription for being blessed, he command us to be like salt. Matthew 5:13-16 "*Ye are the salt of the earth: but if the salt have lost his savour, wherewith shall it be salted? it is thenceforth good for nothing, but to be cast out, and to be trodden under foot of men. Ye are the light of the world. A city that is set on an hill cannot be hid. Neither do men light a candle, and put it under a bushel, but on a candlestick; and it giveth light unto all that are in the house. Let your light so shine before men, that they may see your good works, and glorify your Father which is in heaven.*" Jesus let us know that if we are too busy or too lazy to be a witness then we are good for nothing. We are to make the world thirsty for Jesus.

The miracle of the healing of the waters sets a pattern showing the type of ministry that God is going to use Elisha in. He sets a course of one who brings blessing to those who are living Godly. It also demonstrates the healing power which God worked through Elisha to those who ask him for help. Many times saints in the church miss out on blessing because they do not go to their Pastor and seek his counsel. There is an anointing and Spiritual Gifts that were given him by God to bless the church. 1 Timothy 4:14 "*Neglect not the gift that is in thee, which was given thee by prophecy, with the laying on of the hands of the presbytery.*" Don't cut your Spiritual walk with God short by not allowing your Pastor to edify you with the Spiritual Gifts that are working in his ministry.

Your Pastor is placed in your life by God and he will give an account to God on how you respond to him. Hebrews 13:17 *"Obey them that have the rule over you, and submit yourselves: for they watch for your souls, as they that must give account, that they may do it with joy, and not with grief: for that is unprofitable for you."* I have never seen a dentist chasing a patient down the street begging them to let him pull their tooth. But I know of plenty of people who have called up the dentist and begged him to pull their tooth today. Why wait till we have made a mess of it to seek Godly counsel? If you have never traveled a particular road before then you will be blessed to seek Godly counsel before you start the journey. On the other hand, all of you that know what to do and did the opposite will not be blessed. It will do you no good to go to your Pastor and make excuses for your rebellion or to blame him for your failure. Just go to the altar and repent and get up and clean up your mess and do it right next time.

Judgement At Bethel

> 2 Kings 2:23-24 *"And he went up from thence unto Bethel: and as he was going up by the way, there came forth little children out of the city, and mocked him, and said unto him, Go up, thou bald head; go up, thou bald head. 24 And he turned back, and looked on them, and cursed them in the name of the LORD. And there came forth two she bears out of the wood, and tare forty and two children of them."*

Bethel which means the "House of God" was a place in Central Palestine, about 10 miles north of Jerusalem, at the head of the pass of Michmash and Ai. It was originally the Canaanite city of Luz. The name Bethel was at first apparently given to the sanctuary in the neighborhood of Luz, and was not given to the city itself till after its conquest by the tribe of Ephraim. Bethel is also where God appeared to Jacob (Israel) and he set up a stone for a pillar and called it the House of God. In times of trouble people went to Bethel to ask counsel of God (Judges 20:18 &

21:2). The Ark of the Covenant was kept for a long time under the care of Phinehas, the grandson of Aaron at Bethel (Judges 20:26). Also Samuel held his court of justice at certain times in Bethel (1 Samuel 7:16). After Solomon it became a seat of gross idolatry. King Jeroboam chose it as the place for one of his golden calves. God often sent prophets to preach at Bethel. Many of these prophets pronounced judgment and condemnation on Bethel as a center of idolatry.

Not all of the Bible will fit in with the political correct crowd of today. Too often carnal people and critics of the Bible love to misrepresent what the Bible says in 2 Kings 2:23-24. The way many interpret this text is: innocent teasing by little children was blown way out of proportion by a cranky old prophet who was sensitive about his bald head and was way out of touch with the younger generation. So he shows how cruel and mean he and God is by causing harm to innocent children. The Bible receives open ridicule for this passage by many of the heathens in our society today. We need to pray and study so we will have the right answers if we are ever challenged about this miracle.

What happen at Bethel when a gang of ruffians who were ridiculing, mocking and rejecting God and His prophet was the promised judgement of God on rebellious youth. Leviticus 26:21-25 *"And if ye walk contrary unto me, and will not hearken unto me; I will bring seven times more plagues upon you according to your sins. <u>I will also send wild beasts among you, which shall rob you of your children,</u> and destroy your cattle, and make you few in number; and your high ways shall be desolate. And if ye will not be reformed by me by these things, but will walk contrary unto me; Then will I also walk contrary unto you, and will punish you yet seven times for your sins. And I will bring a sword upon you, that shall avenge the quarrel of my covenant: and when ye are gathered together within your cities, I will send the pestilence among you; and ye shall be delivered into the hand of the enemy."* In Bible times youth up to twenty years of age could be called children (Numbers 1:3). Bethel was one of the worst places in the corrupt and decadent nation of Israel. Bethel should have been a holy place but was a center of idolatry and immorality where the sons of the prophets were vastly outnumbered by those who taunted and trashed the faith of Elijah and Elisha. Bethel was so corrupt that a gang of young teenagers mocked and ridiculed Elisha and probably meant to do him harm. They were a large roving band of teenagers just as dangerous as the large youth gangs that roam the ghetto sections of our modern American cities. They taunted him to leave them and their town alone and go off into the clouds to be with his God as Elijah had done. They did not believe that God had translated Elijah but was making fun of the ideal as being preposterous. God sent a strong message to the city and parents foretelling of even greater judgement to come. This judgement was a warning to the parents and community to repent of their sins. The evil of the parents had brought forth evil in their children and judgement upon their children. It was a warning to obey God before worse judgments was poured out upon them. It is ironic that the she bear which is known as the animal which loves her babies (Hosea 13:8) is the instrument used of God to destroy the youth of the wicked. The evil people of Bethel did not teach their youth to honor the man of God which proves that they did not love their children. If we love our children we are going to take them to the house of God and teach them His ways. So many today are sacrificing their children on the altars of worldly entertainment because they are too busy or lazy to spend time with their children. If we turn our children loose on the internet then we should not be shocked when the evil and perversions of this world consumes them. You are their parents and you are responsible for what they see, hear and do. Psalms 101:3a "*I will set no wicked thing before mine eyes...*" Children are very easily influenced by the words they hear, the videos they watch, the friends they keep and the heroes they follow. If any of these promote sin and rebellion they will have a very negative impact on your children. 1 Corinthians 15:33 "*Be not deceived: evil communications corrupt good manners.*" This is a constant battle which must be fought anew every week. Don't believe you can address these issues one time and it will be resolved. You must be vigilant and go back and look for holes in your defenses quite often. It is only by applying a constant flood of Love, God, prayer, Bible study, church and more church that you will be victorious. Don't forget, you must be the one who teaches your child how to worship God. They will learn by your example.

The attack by bears shows God trying to bring His people back to Him through smaller judgments so that they could avoid a worse long term judgment. The world we live in today is in a headlong dash to the fires of hell. Let us hope and pray the plagues of our day will wake them up before it is too late. Revelation 20:15 *"And whosoever was not found written in the book of life was cast into the lake of fire."*

Jesus Is The Remedy

In miracle two we saw a curse being removed because of Godly men seeking after God to bless their city and asking the prophet for his guidance. In miracle three we saw a curse being placed at an ungodly city with the immediate judgement of it being carried out. God is a God of mercy and grace but he is also a God of Judgement. God is not mocked. Repent and allow the blood of Jesus to wash away your sins while there is still time.

One of the beautiful benefits of Calvary is the fact that God can now make an exchange for some of the crops we have reaped through sin and turn them into a blessing. Isaiah 61:1-4 *"The Spirit of the Lord GOD is upon me; because the LORD hath anointed me to preach good tidings unto the meek; he hath sent me to bind up the brokenhearted, to proclaim liberty to the captives, and the opening of the prison to them that are bound; To proclaim the acceptable year of the LORD, and the day of vengeance of our God; to comfort all that mourn; To appoint unto them that mourn in Zion, to give unto them beauty for ashes, the oil of joy for mourning, the garment of praise for the spirit of heaviness; that they might be called trees of righteousness, the planting of the LORD, that he might be glorified. And they shall build the old wastes, they shall raise up the former desolations, and they shall repair the waste cities, the desolations of many generations."* Jesus is the only door to salvation and we can only come to Him by repenting of our sins and being baptized in the name of Jesus. Then we are promised to be filled with His Spirit which is the Holy Ghost (Acts 2:38).

Discussion Questions

1.   Why is it set in the hearts of man to do evil?

____

____

____

2.   What is a Biblical curse?

____

____

____

3.   Why should we go to our Pastor for help?

____

____

____

4.   What happens when you mock God?

____

____

____

5.   Can a curse be removed?

____

____

____

DOUBLE PORTION
The Miracles Of Elisha

Lesson Four

Living In The Shadow

At first glance this seems to be the story of a battle to be fought by a mixture of kings and kingdoms who were having problems obeying God. On the way to battle they realize that they need God to help them stay alive much less win the battle. On closer examination we find the story is more about a prophet stepping out of the shadows of his predecessor and stepping up to the plate to deliver a lifesaving undeniable miracle that the whole world cannot help but notice. Galatians 6:9 *"And let us not be weary in well doing: for in due season we shall reap, if we faint not."* You are not alone in wondering if you will ever get full credit for your labor, while forgetting all the times when you were splashing in the overflow puddle of your Pastor's anointing and taking credit for the rain. But the day and time will come when God will make full proof of your ministry and if you are called to be a Pastor, God will put the whole responsibility of the church upon your shoulders. 2 Timothy 4:2-5 *"Preach the word; be instant in season, out of season; reprove, rebuke, exhort with all longsuffering and doctrine. For the time will come when they will not endure sound doctrine; but after their own lusts shall they heap to themselves teachers, having itching ears; And they shall turn away their ears from the truth, and shall be turned unto fables. But watch thou in all things, endure afflictions, do the work of an evangelist, make full proof of thy ministry."* Do not be tempted to take a shortcut. Follow in the footsteps of your Pastor until he hands the mantle of anointing over to you. To wield power without authority always ends in disaster. Even after your Pastor has placed you in a position of authority it will take time for people to trust you and for God to prove you. At first you will be living in the shadow.

I am still amazed at how much more can be done when everyone doesn't care who gets the credit or stands in the limelight. Let the church world have their flesh parades and vain glory rallies but let the church be so invisible that all the world can see is Jesus. Let us make way for the next generation to be used of God. What they need are opportunities to test their wings. They will not fly very high at first but the day will come when they are needed and they will be ready to go. The only way they can become skillful in the Word is to be exercised therein. Hebrews 5:12-14 *"For when for the time ye ought to be teachers, ye have need that one teach you again which be the first principles of the oracles of God; and are become such as have need of milk, and not of strong meat. For every one that useth milk is unskilful in the word of righteousness: for he is a babe. But strong meat belongeth to them that are of full age, even those who by reason of use have their senses exercised to discern both good and evil."*

Oh how easy it is to tell others the decisions they should make when we have never had to reap the consequences of those irreversible actions. We are dealing with the souls of mankind and we must do it with longsuffering kindness. So much harm has been done by those who step out of their place and try to enforce the standards the Pastor has set in the Church. May we find our place in the body and stay there until it is time for the Lord to lift us up. James 4:5-6,10 *"Do ye think that the scripture saith in vain, The spirit that dwelleth in us lusteth to envy? But he giveth more grace. Wherefore he saith, God resisteth the proud, but giveth grace unto the humble… Humble yourselves in the sight of the Lord, and he shall lift you up."* God will always deal on the honest hearts and help them find the right path when the time is right. Let us not choke the babes with meat that they cannot handle but let us shower them with the milk of love and kindness.

Scripture Text

2 Kings 3:11-24 *"But Jehoshaphat said, Is there not here a prophet of the LORD, that we may enquire of the LORD by him? And one of the king of Israel's servants answered and said, Here is Elisha the son of Shaphat, which poured water on the hands of Elijah. 12 And Jehoshaphat said, The word of the LORD is with him. So the king of Israel and Jehoshaphat and the king of Edom went down to him. 13 And Elisha said unto the king of Israel, What have I to do with thee? get thee to the prophets of thy father, and to the prophets of thy mother. And the king of Israel said unto him, Nay: for the LORD hath called these three kings together, to deliver them into the hand of Moab. 14 And Elisha said, As the LORD of hosts liveth, before whom I stand, surely, were it not that I regard the presence of Jehoshaphat the king of Judah, I would not look toward thee, nor see thee. 15 But now bring me a minstrel. And it came to pass, when the minstrel played, that the hand of the LORD came upon him. 16 And he said, Thus saith the LORD, Make this valley full of ditches. 17 For thus saith the LORD, Ye shall not see wind, neither shall ye see rain; yet that valley shall be filled with water, that ye may drink, both ye, and your cattle, and your beasts. 18 And this is but a light thing in the sight of the LORD: he will deliver the Moabites also into your hand. 19 And ye shall smite every fenced city, and every choice city, and shall fell every good tree, and stop all wells of water, and mar every good piece of land with stones. 20 And it came to pass in the morning, when the meat offering was offered, that, behold, there came water by the way of Edom, and the country was filled with water. 21 And when all the Moabites heard that the kings were come up to fight against them, they gathered all that were able to put on armour, and upward, and stood in the border. 22 And they rose up early in the morning, and the sun shone upon the water, and the Moabites saw the water on the other side as red as blood: 23 And they said, This is blood: the kings are surely slain, and they have smitten one another: now therefore, Moab, to the spoil. 24 And when they came to the camp of Israel, the Israelites rose up and smote the Moabites, so that they fled before them: but they went forward smiting the Moabites, even in their country."*

The Setting

2 Kings 3:5 "But it came to pass, when Ahab was dead, that the king of Moab rebelled against the king of Israel."

The first player is King Mesha of Moab. King Mesha of Moab was a sheepmaster, and rendered unto the king of Israel an hundred thousand lambs, and an hundred thousand rams, with the wool each year as tribute. The Moabites were the offspring of Lot's son which he had by his eldest daughter. They lived in a territory to the southeast of Judah and east of the Red Sea. They had mighty men and were feared by the Canaanites (Exodus 15:15). They worshiped idols (1 Kings 11:33). King David had brought the Moabites into subjection. They had paid a heavy annual tribute for at least a hundred and fifty years, but upon the death of King Ahab and Queen Jezebel they had decided to throw off the yoke and pay tribute no longer.

The second player is King Jehoram of the divided nation of Israel. King Jehoram wrought evil in the sight of the LORD; but not like his father King Ahab or his mother Queen Jezebel: for he put away the image of Baal that his father had made. Nevertheless he cleaved unto the sins of King Jeroboam the son of Nebat, which was the first king of the divided nation and made Israel to sin. King Jehoram departed not from the sins of King Jeroboam. King Jehoram did not turn to the Lord for counsel and help. King Jehoram should have turned to God now that the Moabites had rebelled. But he was alienated from God. He did not consult the priests of the idols, so apparently he had no faith in them either. How miserable is the life of the sinner in the hour of need, no comfort in the time of sorrow, no righteous counsel in times of despair, no place to go when the storms of life rage. How hollow and empty is this life when we turn our backs upon the God who created us.

The third player is King Jehoshaphat of Judah. King Jehoshaphat was a God fearing man but also he wavered at times. King Jehoram sent to King Jehoshaphat saying that the king of Moab hath rebelled against him and ask King Jehoshaphat to go with him against Moab to battle. King Jehoshaphat replied that he would go to battle with them against the Moabites. It seems strange that King Jehoshaphat was willing to unite with King Jehoram in this battle. He had united with King Ahab in the past. 2 Chronicles 18:1-3 *"Now Jehoshaphat had riches and honour in abundance, and joined affinity with Ahab. And after certain years he went down to Ahab to Samaria. And Ahab killed sheep and oxen for him in abundance, and for the people that he had with him, and persuaded him to go up with him to Ramothgilead. And Ahab king of Israel said unto Jehoshaphat king of Judah, Wilt thou go with me to Ramothgilead? And he answered him, I am as thou art, and my people as thy people; and we will be with thee in the war."* King Jehoshaphat was then severely rebuked for having joined alliance with King Ahab. 2 Chronicles 19:2 *"And Jehu the son of Hanani the seer went out to meet him, and said to king Jehoshaphat, Shouldest thou help the ungodly, and love them that hate the LORD? therefore is wrath upon thee from before the LORD."* There is no a logical explanation as to why King Jehoshaphat was willing to help Israel this time. Maybe his desire to have a working relationship between the two kingdoms inspired him to do it. The Moabites were a common enemy. This would not be the last time that the Moabites would go to battle with King Jehoshaphat. 2 Chronicles 20:1 *"It came to pass after this also, that the children of Moab, and the children of Ammon, and with them other beside the Ammonites, came against Jehoshaphat to battle."* There is a slight possibility that King Jehoshaphat was deceived by King Jehoram's actions of removing the idol of Baal into thinking that he was going to serve God. His biggest mistake was that he did not seek directions from God after he received the message from King Jehoram.

The fourth player is the king of Edom. The Edomites were under the dominion of Judah and served King Jehoshaphat at this time. The Edomites were the offspring of Esau, who was the son of Isaac and grandson of Abraham. Esau was the twin brother of Jacob (Israel). The Edomites had kings long before Israel had a king. Genesis 36:31 *"And these are the kings that reigned in the land of Edom, before there reigned any king over the children of Israel."* According to the historian Josephus the Edomites worshiped a variety of gods and one of them was named Koze. The Edomites lived in the land south of the Dead Sea. The Edomites had not been kind to the nation of Israel after they had come out of Egypt even though they were blood related.

Numbers 20:14-21 *"And Moses sent messengers from Kadesh unto the king of Edom, Thus saith thy brother Israel, Thou knowest all the travail that hath befallen us: How our fathers went down into Egypt, and we have dwelt in Egypt a long time; and the Egyptians vexed us, and our fathers: And when we cried unto the LORD, he heard our voice, and sent an angel, and hath brought us forth out of Egypt: and, behold, we are in Kadesh, a city in the uttermost of thy border: Let us pass, I pray thee, through thy country: we will not pass through the fields, or through the vineyards, neither will we drink of the water of the wells: we will go by the king's high way, we will not turn to the right hand nor to the left, until we have passed thy borders. And Edom said unto him, Thou shalt not pass by me, lest I come out against thee with the sword. And the children of Israel said unto him, We will go by the high way: and if I and my cattle drink of thy water, then I will pay for it: I will only, without doing any thing else, go through on my feet. And he said, Thou shalt not go through. And Edom came out against him with much people, and with a strong hand. Thus Edom refused to give Israel passage through his border: wherefore Israel turned away from him."* During the reign of King David he had made them servants and at the time of this miracle they were servants to King Jehoshaphat. 2 Samuel 8:14 *"And he put garrisons in Edom; throughout all Edom put he garrisons, and all they of Edom became David's servants. And the LORD preserved David whithersoever he went."* While the people of God served him, they ruled over their enemies. After the death of King Jehoshaphat the Edomites rebelled against his son (an evil king) and made themselves a king. 2 Chronicles 21:8 *"In his days the Edomites revolted from under the dominion of Judah, and made themselves a king."*

The fifth player is the Prophet Elisha. Elisha means "God is Savior" and his father's name Shaphat means "judge." He was living in Abel-meholah when Elijah called him into the ministry. Abel-meholah means "meadow of the dance" and was a place in the inheritance of the tribe of Issachar, at the north of the Jordan valley. Elisha's father Shaphat was a man of some means for he had "twelve yoke of oxen" engaged in plowing when Elisha was called. Shaphat did not allow his son to be lazy as is so often the case with the wealthy. It was while Elisha was working that he was called to be a Prophet. Elisha's acceptance of this call not only meant the giving up of a comfortable wealthy lifestyle but the leaving of home and family. Elijah was very far from being a popular person in the nation of Israel. He had powerful enemies which included the king and queen and they had upon more than one occasion tried to take his life. Danger, persecution and sacrifice were not only a possibility but a probability. The evil Queen Jezebel and her government persecuted Elijah. The same situations face the ministry today. The truth is despised and rejected of men. To be preaching and teaching the truth will bring hostility not only from the secular world but also from the religious world we live in. But the greatest enemy of the truth today is the false prophets who called themselves Christians. 2 Timothy 4:3-4 *"For the time will come when they will not endure sound doctrine; but after their own lusts shall they heap to themselves teachers, having itching ears; And they shall turn away their ears from the truth, and shall be turned unto fables."* The call upon Elisha was confirmed by the prophet Elijah casting his mantle upon him. This call brought with it the power and anointing of God. After Elisha became a Prophet, he lived in Samaria. Samaria was the capital of the nation of Israel and where the backslidden king and people of the divided kingdom lived. By living in Samaria, Elisha manifested his readiness to be used of God as He saw fit. Samaria was a gloomy and tough field of labor because it was ruled by a king who had turned his back upon God. Even though Elisha had already preformed three mighty miracles, the kings of the land did not know that he existed. As we see this lesson unfold, we will see how God allows Elisha to find favor, honor and recognition as the man of God with multiple kings in his world. This reminds us of how Joseph found favor wherever he went and brought blessing upon their establishments. Genesis 39:21 *"But the LORD was with Joseph, and shewed him mercy, and gave him favour in the sight of the keeper of the prison."*

The Looming Disaster

2 Kings 3:9 *"So the king of Israel went, and the king of Judah, and the king of Edom: and they fetched a compass of seven days' journey: and there was no water for the host, and for the cattle that followed them."*

Here are the armies of Israel, Judah and Edom after they had taken the long way around the wilderness into Moab in order to surprise their enemy and it took seven days. Their armies would have consisted of soldiers, horses and pack animals. They were now dying of thirst because the oases had dried up. This became a seriously situation with no possible solution but to die of thirst. They could not go back, they would die before they got home. They could not go forward, the Moabites would kill them. They could not stay there because they had no water. There was no way or no one left to bring them water. It is when we get to the end of our road that we have arrived in God's front yard and now he can begin to do his business. We all will experience what seems like impossible situations and the only solution is help from above. You will be at the end of your rope, your experience, your education, your family, your money, your government, and medical science will all fail you. Now the only thing that can save you is for God to act. There will always come times in our lives when we will know that only God can act in this situation. It was only God who could make it rain. To the armies of Israel, Judah and Edom it didn't matter how many troops they had, it didn't matter how many horses they had or how much food they had, without water they could not go on. When we find ourselves in an impossible situation we need to remember to fall to our knees and ask God to do what only God can do. Hebrews 4:16 *"Let us therefore come boldly unto the throne of grace, that we may obtain mercy, and find grace to help in time of need."*

The Shadow Is Cast

> 2 Kings 3:11 *"But Jehoshaphat said, Is there not here a prophet of the LORD, that we may enquire of the LORD by him? And one of the king of Israel's servants answered and said, Here is Elisha the son of Shaphat, which poured water on the hands of Elijah."*

Let us take notice that King Jehoram did not speak about Elisha but it was one of his servants that had heard of him. When the mighty name of the Prophet Elijah is spoken, everyone knows who you are talking about. But Elisha is still identified as the son of a successful man, given no credit for any accomplishments of his own. He is just the water boy of the great and deceased Prophet Elijah. How easy would it have been for Elisha to despair and walk away from his calling at this point. It looks like he will never get out from under the shadow of Elijah and be respected and accredited for the work he was doing. No one knows who he is and he is only being called in as a last resort because they are desperate. They also expect him to go out into the middle of a desert where everyone is dying of thirst to die with them or perform a miracle. Why would anyone want to work under these circumstances?

How many of you today have heard the enemy whisper in your ear; you might as well give up because you are never going to amount to anything? Everywhere you look someone else is getting credit for your labors. All the good jobs are being given to the people with a name and a heritage. No one will even give you one small chance. It seems like you are pounding upon a rock with a foam hammer while everyone else is given dynamite to blast with. There will even be times when those who are younger than you are revered by the people. 1 Samuel 18:8 *"And Saul was very wroth, and the saying displeased him; and he said, They have ascribed unto David ten thousands, and to me they have ascribed but thousands: and what can he have more but the kingdom?"* How are you going to respond?

The Minstrel

> 2 Kings 3:15 *"But now bring me a minstrel. And it came to pass, when the minstrel played, that the hand of the LORD came upon him."*

What does Elisha do when he is presented with the problem? He asks for them to bring him one of the sons of the prophets so he can play and they can sing praises unto God. We need to make sure that we understand what is going on here, this is a very serious situation. We have three armies in the middle of a desert, who have ran out of water after seven grueling days of marching. After hearing this news the Prophet Elisha wants to have a praise and worship service. Acts 16:25-30 *"And at midnight Paul and Silas prayed, and sang praises unto God: and the prisoners heard them. And suddenly there was a great earthquake, so that the foundations of the prison were shaken: and immediately all the doors were opened, and every one's bands were loosed. And the keeper of the prison awaking out of his sleep, and seeing the prison doors open, he drew out his sword, and would have killed himself, supposing that the prisoners had been fled. But Paul cried with a loud voice, saying, Do thyself no harm: for we are all here. Then he called for a light, and sprang in, and came trembling, and fell down before Paul and Silas, And brought them out, and said, Sirs, what must I do to be saved?"* When we begin to praise God the foundations of evil will be shaken. The world would definitely be wondering what is going on here. What we need to realize is that music is the gateway to the spirit world and that is why it is so important to praise and worship during our trials, during our victories and everywhere in-between. Also we need to realize that the wrong kind of music can open up the gates of hell and begin to spew evil into our lives. There is demons attached to worldly music. Godly music will usher us into the presence of God. What the world sees as improbable is just the ticket to get the victory party rolling.

The Small Miracle

> 2 Kings 3:16-18 *"And he said, Thus saith the LORD, Make this valley full of ditches. 17 For thus saith the LORD, Ye shall not see wind, neither shall ye see rain; yet that valley shall be filled with water, that ye may drink, both ye, and your cattle, and your beasts. 18 And this is but a light thing in the sight of the LORD: he will deliver the Moabites also into your hand."*

After they had got done with their shouting and dancing, then Elisha continues with the improbable by telling them to "dig ditches." They had marched in the hot desert for seven days and all the oases they had come to were found all dried up and now he expected them to dig ditches. What good are ditches if you have no water? Living for God is like digging ditches in the desert. Living for God often feels like work without reward or credit for our labors until the day of harvest. Living for God is often hard work with no shortcuts. Living for God seems crazy to carnal people. Living for God sometimes is done without an answer in sight, just a walk of faith. The armies never saw the rain fall or saw the wind blow. There can be times that we need miracles to help us continue our journey to heaven. God does not always preform the same miracle for you that he has done for others. He may provide for you in a different way. Many are willing to forsake the miraculous to depend upon their own abilities. But in the end your own abilities will fail you. Living for God must be guided by the preaching and teaching of the Word. Living for God is blessed beyond expectation if we will not become weary in well doing. Galatians 6:7-9 *"Be not deceived; God is not mocked: for whatsoever a man soweth, that shall he also reap. For he that soweth to his flesh shall of the flesh reap corruption; but he that soweth to the Spirit shall of the Spirit reap life everlasting. And let us not be weary in well doing: for in due season we shall reap, if we faint not."* Living for God is like digging ditches in the desert.

Go For Total Victory

2 Kings 3:19 *"And ye shall smite every fenced city, and every choice city, and shall fell every good tree, and stop all wells of water, and mar every good piece of land with stones."*

Sometimes we are content to settle for the ordinary when God wants us to go for total victory. Don't underestimate the power of God. When the time comes, God is going to go BIG. It is not enough to drive the enemy out of your yard today, just to have him come back tomorrow. God wants you to defeat that enemy so that we will never come back again. I am talking total deliverance here. Get the victory over that trial and never look back. When God got done with the Moabites they would never forget the Prophet Elisha. The armies ravaged the countryside of the Moabites taking spoils. Tore down the fences and walls, leveled the main villages, clear cut the fruit and nut orchards, stop up the springs and filled up the wells, and cluttered the cultivated fields with stones to make plowing impossible. Later on we will study about the tragedy of partial victory.

The Ripples On The Water Brings the Big Miracle

2 Kings 3:20-24 *"And it came to pass in the morning, when*

the meat offering was offered, that, behold, there came water by the way of Edom, and the country was filled with water. 21 And when all the Moabites heard that the kings were come up to fight against them, they gathered all that were able to put on armour, and upward, and stood in the border. 22 And they rose up early in the morning, and the sun shone upon the water, and the Moabites saw the water on the other side as red as blood: 23 And they said, This is blood: the kings are surely slain, and they have smitten one another: now therefore, Moab, to the spoil. 24 And when they came to the camp of Israel, the Israelites rose up and smote the Moabites, so that they fled before them: but they went forward smiting the Moabites, even in their country."

It happened just as Elisha said it would. They dug ditches, a flash flood swept across the desert, the water was saved in the ditches, and they were saved from dying of thirst. Without the ditches the water would have passed them by and they would still have been thirsty. The water that brought their salvation became the water that was used to defeat the Moabites. Our enemy saw the blood of Calvary as the symbol of defeat but it because the symbol of deliverance by washing away all our sins. It is interesting to note that the plan of the kings to surprise the Moabites did not work. The Moabites were at their border waiting for them to arrive. It does not matter how much we plan, if God is not the author of our plan it will come to naught. James 4:13-17 *"Go to now, ye that say, To day or to morrow we will go into such a city, and continue there a year, and buy and sell, and get gain: Whereas ye know not what shall be on the morrow. For what is your life? It is even a vapour, that appeareth for a little time, and then vanisheth away. For that ye ought to say, If the Lord will, we shall live, and do this, or that. But now ye rejoice in your boastings: all such rejoicing is evil. Therefore to him that knoweth to do good, and doeth it not, to him it is sin."* This once again shows us how important Godly counsel is, if we want to succeed. The water in the ditches became a means of confusion and defeat to the enemy. What the Moabites saw as death was in actuality the water of life. Many look at holiness as bondage when actually it is freedom from sin. How many times have you got in trouble when you jumped to a conclusion without all the facts? We live in a generation that is offended way to easy. Have you ever heard of suffering wrong for the Kingdom of God sake?   James 1:19-20 "*Wherefore, my beloved brethren, let every man be swift to hear, slow to speak, slow to wrath: For the wrath of man worketh not the righteousness of God.*"   The Lord delivered the Moabites unto the hands of the Israelites. It is time that we let the Lord fight our battles for us.

The Established Prophet

What a contrast these miracles provide us with. Elijah had been a prophet that spent his life running from King Ahab and Queen Jezebel and now Elisha has just saved three kingdoms from annihilations and has the undying gratitude of kings. Elisha's work is far from done but God has opened up new doors of opportunity for him to walk through.   We should never look at mountain top experiences as a final destination but should consider them as the place where our real work has begun. There are many who can conquer but there are few who then can govern in peace. Just remember, sometimes it is lonely at the top. To be the one who has to administer correction can be a heart wrenching job.   Titus 1:7-13 "*For a bishop must be blameless, as the steward of God; not selfwilled, not soon angry, not given to wine, no striker, not given to filthy lucre; But a lover of hospitality, a lover of good men, sober, just, holy, temperate; Holding fast the faithful word as he hath been taught, that he may be able by sound doctrine both to exhort and to convince the gainsayers. For there are many unruly and vain talkers and deceivers, specially they of the circumcision: Whose mouths must be stopped, who subvert whole houses, teaching things which they ought not, for filthy lucre's sake. One of themselves, even a prophet of their own, said, The Cretians are alway liars, evil beasts, slow bellies. This witness is true. <u>Wherefore rebuke them sharply</u>, that they may be sound in the faith.*" Every victory has a purpose.   The victory of Jesus at Calvary has now opened the door for us to preach the gospel (Act 2:38) to every lost sinner in the world. Let us all go forth and fulfill our call.

Discussion Questions

1. Who is it that can eat strong meat?

____

____

____

2. What happens if we are not weary in well doing?

____

____

____

3. What happens when we begin to worship God?

____

____

____

4. What happens when we rebuke without authority?

____

____

____

5. What was Elisha doing when he was called to be a prophet?

____

____

____

DOUBLE PORTION
The Miracles Of Elisha

Lesson Five

The Multiplier

We serve a God who adds, multiplies and builds up his children. The children of the world serve a god who subtracts, divides and tears down his children. If we will serve God with a whole heart we will find our days filled with blessings. One of the great benefits of the Kingdom of God is peace. The world we live in today is full of depression, anger and regret. Proverbs 3:1-7 "*My son, forget not my law; but let thine heart keep my commandments: For length of days, and long life, and peace, shall they add to thee. Let not mercy and truth forsake thee: bind them about thy neck; write them upon the table of thine heart: So shalt thou find favour and good understanding in the sight of God and man. Trust in the LORD with all thine heart; and lean not unto thine own understanding. In all thy ways acknowledge him, and he shall direct thy paths. Be not wise in thine own eyes: fear the LORD, and depart from evil.*" When we look at our material possession they may seem meager. When we access our talents they may seem scant. When we examine our influence it may seem very limited. When we count our money it may fall short. There are even times when our friends may seem few and far away. But we serve a God who is the multiplier! He specializes in taking the little and astounding the masses with how great he can make it. God just wants us to bring Him what we have and let him begin to multiply it. All we need is the blessings of God. Yes, there will be times that our faith is tested. We will have given all that we have and more to do the work of God and then we find ourselves in need. Hebrews 4:16 *"Let us therefore come boldly unto the throne of grace, that we may obtain mercy, and find grace to help in time of need."* When we come to God with a whole heart we will never hear Him say; that is not enough. It is those who hold something back that always leave disappointed because God will not accept a halfhearted offering.

How can people not realize how empty they will become when they serve the gods of this world? Haggai 1:5-6 *"Now therefore thus saith the LORD of hosts; Consider your ways. Ye have sown much, and bring in little; ye eat, but ye have not enough; ye drink, but ye are not filled with drink; ye clothe you, but there is none warm; and he that earneth wages earneth wages to put it into a bag with holes."* No matter how great a man possessions are in this world, they are never enough to satisfy his lust. They will always live in fear of losing what they have because they serves the subtractor. In the long run the enemy makes every situation miserable, he will never help you, he is always negative and brings calamities. All the while he is trying to rock you to sleep with the endless parade of material possession that are here today and gone tomorrow. Romans 13:11-14 *"And that, knowing the time, that now it is high time to awake out of sleep: for now is our salvation nearer than when we believed. The night is far spent, the day is at hand: let us therefore cast off the works of darkness, and let us put on the armour of light. Let us walk honestly, as in the day; not in rioting and drunkenness, not in chambering and wantonness, not in strife and envying. But put ye on the Lord Jesus Christ, and make not provision for the flesh, to fulfil the lusts thereof."* No matter how much man tries to satisfy the lust of the flesh, it can never be done. Lust will always take you deeper and deeper into the previsions of sin. But just like drug additions, lust always seeks greater perversions just to satisfy the appetite of yesterday. When the day is done you are left cold, lonely and miserable with no hope for a better tomorrow. Then you wind up watching others enjoy the fruits of your labor while you are left lonely and forsaken.

Scripture Text

2 Kings 4:1-7 *"Now there cried a certain woman of the wives of the sons of the prophets unto Elisha, saying, Thy servant my husband is dead; and thou knowest that thy servant did fear the LORD: and the creditor is come to take unto him my two sons to be bondmen. 2 And Elisha said unto her, What shall I do for thee? tell me, what hast thou in the house? And she said, Thine handmaid hath not any thing in the house, save a pot of oil. 3 Then he said, Go, borrow thee vessels abroad of all thy neighbours, even empty vessels; borrow not a few. 4 And when thou art come in, thou shalt shut the door upon thee and upon thy sons, and shalt pour out into all those vessels, and thou shalt set aside that which is full. 5 So she went from him, and shut the door upon her and upon her sons, who brought the vessels to her; and she poured out. 6 And it came to pass, when the vessels were full, that she said unto her son, Bring me yet a vessel. And he said unto her, There is not a vessel more. And the oil stayed. 7 Then she came and told the man of God. And he said, Go, sell the oil, and pay thy debt, and live thou and thy children of the rest."*

A Look At History

According to the Targum, Chaldee, Jarchi, the rabbis and the historian Josephus, this woman was the wife of Obadiah the former governor of the house of King Ahab and Queen Jezebel. We first see Obadiah being called by King Ahab to help him look for grass to feed the horses and mules. Because God had honored a request of the Prophet Elijah, it had not rained in the land of Israel for over three years and they had run out of food for the livestock. 1 Kings 17:1 *"And Elijah the Tishbite, who was of the inhabitants of Gilead, said unto Ahab, As the LORD God of Israel liveth, before whom I stand, there shall not be dew nor rain these years, but according to my word."* So Obadiah was off to look throughout the land at all the springs, brooks and wells trying to find some grass for the livestock. They were in danger of losing the remainder of the beast that were left alive after three years of no rain or dew. As Obadiah was on his journey, Elijah met him. Of course Obadiah knew who Elijah was and showed him great honor. The request that Elijah had for Obadiah at first appeared to Obadiah as a suicide mission. Obadiah even asked Elijah if it was because of a sin that he had committed that he was requested to do the impossible. He then begins to explain to Elijah why there was no way he could carry out the request and live. 1 Kings 18:1-16 "*And it came to pass after many days, that the word of the LORD came to Elijah in the third year, saying, Go, shew thyself unto Ahab; and I will send rain upon the earth. And Elijah went to shew himself unto Ahab. And there was a sore famine in Samaria. And Ahab called Obadiah, which was the governor of his house. (Now Obadiah feared the LORD greatly: For it was so, when Jezebel cut off the prophets of the LORD, that Obadiah took an hundred prophets, and hid them by fifty in a cave, and fed them with bread and water.) And Ahab said unto Obadiah, Go into the land, unto all fountains of water, and unto all brooks: peradventure we may find grass to save the horses and mules alive, that we lose not all the beasts. So they divided the land between them to pass throughout it: Ahab went onc way by himself, and Obadiah went another way by himself. And as Obadiah was in the way, behold, Elijah met him: and he knew him, and fell on his face, and said, Art thou that my lord Elijah? And he answered him, I am: go, tell thy lord, Behold, Elijah is here. And he said, What have I sinned, that thou wouldest deliver thy servant into the hand of Ahab, to slay me? As the LORD thy God liveth, there is no nation or kingdom, whither my lord hath not sent to seek thee: and when they said, He is not there; he took an oath of the kingdom and nation, that they found thee not. And now thou sayest, Go, tell thy lord, Behold, Elijah is here. And it shall come to pass, as soon as I am gone from thee, that the Spirit of the LORD shall carry thee whither I know not; and so when I come and tell Ahab, and he cannot find thee, he shall slay me: but I thy servant fear the LORD from my youth. Was it not told my lord what I did when Jezebel slew the prophets of the LORD, how I hid an hundred men of the LORD'S prophets by fifty in a cave, and fed them with bread and water? And now thou sayest, Go, tell thy lord, Behold, Elijah is here: and he shall slay me. And Elijah said, As the LORD of hosts liveth, before whom I stand, I will surely shew myself unto him to day. So Obadiah went to meet Ahab, and told him: and Ahab went to meet Elijah.*"

At the first mention of Obadiah's name in the Word of God it tells us that he was a man who feared the Lord greatly. Our lesson text today confirms the fact that the widow's husband did fear the Lord.

This is the only layman mentioned in First and Second Kings who feared the Lord. So this is a strong point in favor of the history we find telling us that the widow's husband was Obadiah. When Jezebel cut off the prophets of the LORD, Obadiah took an hundred prophets, and hid them by fifty in caves, and fed them with bread and water. So we see that Obadiah was actively involved with the sons of the prophets and saved the life of one hundred of them with great expense to himself. History tells us at some point he was dismissed from the position of governor and went to work at the School of the Prophets. So this would make Obadiah considered as one of the sons of the prophets. When Elijah meet Obadiah he called himself the servant of the prophet. The widow called her husband the servant of the prophet bringing credence to him being Obadiah and working at the School of the Prophets. Elisha was the head of the schools at this time making him responsible for them. In the beginning Obadiah started out with wealth and great material possessions. But the great expense of feeding one hundred men in a time of famine depleted his wealth and forced him to borrow money in order to continue to feed the sons of the prophets. Elisha or the School of the Prophets did not receive money from the priesthood or Levites. Their support came from the Godly people left in the land of Israel. It was from the son of the wicked King Ahab and Queen Jezebel that Obadiah borrowed his money. The son of King Ahab became King Jehoram and was now collecting his debt after the death of Obadiah.

The Fear Of The Lord

The Hebrew verb **yare** can mean "to fear, to respect, to reverence". The Greek noun **phobos** can mean "reverential fear" of God, 'not a mere 'fear' of His power and righteous retribution, but a wholesome dread of displeasing Him". The fear of the Lord will bring:

✦ An attitude that the Lord is worthy of reverence

✦ We will trust; showing respect

✦ Praise Him for His excellent greatness

✦ Will make the Word of God the ultimate authority in our life

✦ We will quit hiding behind ignorance

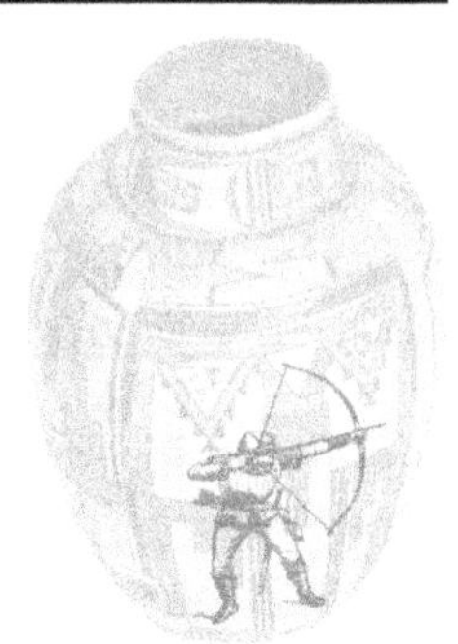

+ We will desire to learn of His holiness

+ We will hate evil and be repulsed by sin

+ We will desire daily fellowship with Him

+ Will eliminate slothfulness

+ It is a fear driven by love and hope

+ Our purpose will become to please God

+ An understanding of judgement and hell

+ The abandonment of excuses

+ A repentance that will bring a change of direction

+ Not a dread of punishment but a desire for blessings

+ Not being careless in our duties

+ It will bring enthusiasm in our worship

+ We will not neglect; tithing, prayer and church attendance

+ Godly fear is not a paralyzing terror

+ Will bring motivation to do good

The mighty men of the Old Testament were known as men that feared the Lord. Joseph was thrust into slavery as a boy and had a journey where he wound up as the ruler of all Egypt. Joseph constantly demonstrated his fear of the Lord. Genesis 42:18 *"And Joseph said unto them the third day, This do, and live; for I fear God."* The man that God had so much confidence in that He allowed the enemy to put him through the fire to prove his love was Job. Job 1:1 *"There was a man in the land of Uz, whose name was Job; and that man was perfect and upright, and one that feared God, and eschewed evil."* Once again we see the overcoming child of God feared Him. What more can we say of Abraham, Moses, David, Samuel and Elijah but that they feared God. The good kings of the Bible (Asa, Jehoshaphat, Jotham, Hezikiah and Josiah) were measured by one thing; they feared the Lord and did what was pleasing in His sight. The same was true for the measure of an evil king; he did not fear God and did what was evil in the sight of the Lord. The same is true for our life today. We must fear the Lord.

The New Testament church had revival and was multiplied when they feared the Lord. Acts 9:31 *"Then had the churches rest throughout all Judaea and Galilee and Samaria, and were edified; and <u>walking in the fear of the Lord</u>, and in the comfort of the Holy Ghost, <u>were multiplied</u>."* Before the multiplication of the Lord can come, the fear of the Lord must come. A church that is living a cavalier lifestyle and is obsessed with materialism will never obtain true revival. Revelation 3:14-19 *"And unto the angel of the church of the Laodiceans write; These things saith the Amen, the faithful and true witness, the beginning of the creation of God; I know thy works, that thou art neither cold nor hot: I would thou wert cold or hot. So then because thou art lukewarm, and neither cold nor hot, I will spue thee out of my mouth. Because thou sayest, I am rich, and increased with goods, and have need of nothing; and knowest not that thou art wretched, and miserable, and poor, and blind, and naked: I counsel thee to buy of me gold tried in the fire, that thou mayest be rich; and white raiment, that thou mayest be clothed, and that the shame of thy nakedness do not appear; and anoint thine eyes with eyesalve, that thou mayest see. As many as I love, I rebuke and chasten: be zealous therefore, and repent."* Living for God is not fire insurance or a get out of jail free card. Living for God is a purpose driven life of righteous, peace and joy provided by working in His Kingdom.

A Tragedy In The Making

> 2 Kings 4:1 *"Now there cried a certain woman of the wives of the sons of the prophets unto Elisha, saying, Thy servant my husband is dead; and thou knowest that thy servant did fear the LORD: and the creditor is come to take unto him my two sons to be bondmen."*

They were not looking at a bad day, they were looking at a bad seven years or more. Not only was the widow bereft of her husband but she was left destitute, in debt and without the means of paying the debt or providing for her family's daily needs. A more abject and sad object could scarcely be conceived. In her miserable plight she went to the head of the School of the Prophets and told him of her desperate situation. Her husband may have died while Elisha was absent with the kings in their expedition against the Moabites, and thus he was unacquainted with her troubles. Sometimes God permits His people to go through trials, this in not always a chastisement because of their slothfulness. This was not a trial brought about because of her wrong doing but rather a place she found herself in because her husband had done the right thing. The Lord sometimes will bring us to the end of our own resources so that His delivering hand may be plainly seen acting on our behalf.

During Old Testament times the prophet was a peculiarity, there was no place or position provided for him by the Law of Moses, no need of him in the religious administration of Israel during ordinary times. The Law of Moses gave him no authority. It was only in seasons of serious moral decline or apostasy that he appeared on the scene. Thus, no stated maintenance was provided for him, as it was for the priests and Levites under the Law of Moses. Consequently the prophet was dependent upon the gifts of those who feared God or the productions of his own manual labors in order to live. Judging from the brief records of the Word of God, one gathers the impression that most of them enjoyed little more than the barest necessities of life. It is possible that the widow's husband obtained part of his subsistence from the oil obtained from an olive grove. Note how readily the widow obtained from her neighbors a lot of empty vessels.

Her creditor was enforcing his demands. He had actually come to seize her sons to be bondmen. The Hebrew word rendered "creditor" in 2 Kings 4:1 signifies "one who exacts what is justly due to him", and is so translated in Job 11:6. What her creditor was trying to do would have been a perverted rendering of the Law of Moses. But we must remember that Israel did not have a God fearing king at this time. Leviticus 25:39-43 *"And if thy brother that dwelleth by thee be waxen poor, and be sold unto thee; thou shalt not compel him to serve as a bondservant: But as an hired servant, and as a sojourner, he shall be with thee, and shall serve thee unto the year of jubile: And then shall he depart from thee, both he and his children with him, and shall return unto his own family, and unto the possession of his fathers shall he return. For they are my servants, which I brought forth out of the land of Egypt: they shall not be sold as bondmen. Thou shalt not rule over him with rigour; but shalt fear thy God."* The widow was in a position where the creditor was intending to break the law and make her sons bondmen, so what would stop him from being tyrannical and abusive or from not setting them free in the year of jubilee?

This was not what God wanted to happen amongst His people. Jesus says it best in this parable. Matthew 18:21-35 *"Then came Peter to him, and said, Lord, how oft shall my brother sin against me, and I forgive him? till seven times? Jesus saith unto him, I say not unto thee, Until seven times: but, Until seventy times seven. Therefore is the kingdom of heaven likened unto a certain king, which would take account of his servants. And when he had begun to reckon, one was brought unto him, which owed him ten thousand talents. But forasmuch as he had not to pay, his lord commanded him to be sold, and his wife, and children, and all that he had, and payment to be made. The servant therefore fell down, and worshipped him, saying, Lord, have patience with me, and I will pay thee all. Then the lord of that servant was moved with compassion, and loosed him, and forgave him the debt. But the same servant went out, and found one of his fellowservants, which owed him an hundred pence: and he laid hands on him, and took him by the throat, saying, Pay me that thou owest. And his fellowservant fell down at his feet, and besought him, saying, Have patience with me, and I will pay thee all. And he would not: but went and cast him into prison, till he should pay the debt. So when his fellowservants saw what was done, they were very sorry, and came and told unto their lord all that was done. Then his lord, after that he had called him, said unto him, O thou wicked servant, I forgave thee all that debt, because thou desiredst me: Shouldest not thou also have had compassion on thy fellowservant, even as I had pity on thee? And his lord was wroth, and delivered him to the tormentors, till he should pay all that was due unto him. So likewise shall my heavenly Father do also unto you, if ye from your hearts forgive not every one his brother their trespasses."*

Allow God To Use What You Got

2 Kings 4:2 *"And Elisha said unto her, What shall I do for thee? tell me, what hast thou in the house? And she said, Thine handmaid hath not any thing in the house, save a pot of oil."*

God was getting ready to perform a miracle but once again was demonstrating His desire to use what we have in order to multiply it into what we need. We may look at ourselves as inadequate and not able to do the job but God sees a vessel He is getting ready to bless. Not only did he fill us with the Holy Ghost but he is in the process of perfecting the saints. Ephesians 4:11-16 *"And he gave some, apostles; and some, prophets; and some, evangelists; and some, pastors and teachers; For the perfecting of the saints, for the work of the ministry, for the edifying of the body of Christ: Till we all come in the unity of the faith, and of the knowledge of the Son of God, unto a perfect man, unto the measure of the stature of the fulness of Christ: That we henceforth be no more children, tossed to and fro, and carried about with every wind of doctrine, by the sleight of men, and cunning craftiness, whereby they lie in wait to deceive; But speaking the truth in love, may grow up into him in all things, which is the head, even Christ: From whom the whole body fitly joined together and compacted by that which every joint supplieth, according to the effectual working in the measure of every part, maketh increase of the body unto the edifying of itself in love."* We are the ones that God is going to use to bring revival to the world in the last days.

Let us not forget the multitude of five thousand men plus women and children who were famished one day after hearing the teaching of Jesus. When Jesus ask for food to feed them the apostle gave up on the task before they ever got started because they only had five loaves and two fishes. They had forgotten that Jesus was the multiplier. Oh that we would bring what we have and give it to Jesus that he might multiply it and supply the needs of our brothers and sisters. But we shoot ourselves in the foot by deciding we are defeated before we ever go to battle. So many look around and decide what their brother has is better and then they try to emulate their brother's call and ministry. What God has called you too and the talents he has given you is what God is going to bless and multiply. You will always be disappointed at the end of the day if you judge you success by what your brother has done. 2 Corinthians 10:12 *"...but they measuring themselves by themselves, and comparing themselves among themselves, are not wise."* Remember there are some that sow the seed and others that water but it is God that gives the increase. To some it is thirty fold to other it is sixty fold and to some an hundred fold but all gave what they had before the increase came.

Go Big Or Go Home

> 2 Kings 4:3 "Then he said, Go, borrow thee vessels abroad of all thy neighbours, even empty vessels; borrow not a few."

It was beyond the powers of Elisha to pay her debt. God chose not to rain down money from heaven. Because they feared God and had been faithful to His service, God planned to provide for them, but there was a test of obedience before the miracle happen. If the widow woman would not have been obedient to the request of the man of God, she would have never seen the miracle of multiplying oil. Are you willing to follow the man of God's instructions? It was a test both of her faith and her obedience. To carnal thinking it would appear that the prophet was only mocking her, for of what possible service could a lot of empty vessels be to her? But if her trust was in the Lord, then she would be willing to submit and comply with the request of the prophet. Are not His thoughts and ways the opposite of the old carnal man? We need to come before the Lord as empty vessels. We need to be emptied of our self-sufficiency if we ever want to experience His wonder working power.

Let us not overlook the good relationship she had with her neighbors. How do we expect to win the lost if we are mean and rude to everyone we meet? We should be known as the nicest and kindest people in town. Go out of your way to win the favor of those who you come in contact with every day. We should never be known as the griper and complainer by our neighbors and coworkers.

When God says to GO BIG, then He means GO BIG! What if she had only borrowed a few vessels? What if we only pray little prayers? What if we only give small offerings? What if we only witness sometimes? What if we only have a little holiness? What if we only read a little of our Bible? What if we only obey our

Pastor sometimes? What if we only go to church when we feel like it? Then we are refusing to GO BIG on the things He has commanded us to GO BIG on and will be left behind. Jeremiah 12:5 *"If thou hast run with the footmen, and they have wearied thee, then how canst thou contend with horses? and if in the land of peace, wherein thou trustedst, they wearied thee, then how wilt thou do in the swelling of Jordan?"*

Some Miracles Require Hard Work

> 2 Kings 4:4-7 *"And when thou art come in, thou shalt shut the door upon thee and upon thy sons, and shalt pour out into all those vessels, and thou shalt set aside that which is full. So she went from him, and shut the door upon her and upon her sons, who brought the vessels to her; and she poured out. And it came to pass, when the vessels were full, that she said unto her son, Bring me yet a vessel. And he said unto her, There is not a vessel more. And the oil stayed. Then she came and told the man of God. And he said, Go, sell the oil, and pay thy debt, and live thou and thy children of the rest."*

She was to shut her door before the oil was poured to avoid flamboyance. When we go to church we are not going for a sensational performance of choreographed actors. Every saint is there to be a part of the praise and worship. Church is not a spectator sport. Church is a place where everyone is to participate in worship to the King of Kings and Lord of Lords. In the pass we have seen charlatans turn the miracle of healing into a circus side show. Time and time again we see false prophets promoting themselves as great workers of miracles. If God does not get the glory then God is not in a hundred miles of it. Miracles happen when something blocks the will of God. Many people get it backwards, believers are not commanded to follow signs and wonders, but God promises that signs and wonders will follow the believers. 1 Corinthians 1:26-29 *"For ye see your calling, brethren, how that not many wise men after the flesh, not many mighty, not many noble, are called: But God hath chosen the foolish things of the world to confound the wise; and God hath chosen the weak things of the world to confound the things which are mighty; And base things of the world, and things which are despised, hath God chosen, yea, and things which are not, to bring to nought things that are: That no flesh should glory in his presence."*

Her neighbors were not a part of the righteous and were not permitted to witness the Lord's gracious dealings with her. It reminds us of Jesus' raising the daughter of Jairus from the dead. When Jesus arrived at the house it was filled with doubting and mocking people and Jesus put them all out (Mark 5:40) before He went in and performed the miracle. The same principle applies today in connection with the working of miracles, the unbelievers will not see the miraculous (Matthew 13:57-58). The moment of the miraculous is not very often accented with flashing lights, a glorious audience and the booming voice of revelation. It is just a moment when all others avenues have been closed and we call to God with faith and trust knowing He will make a way. It can be a simple and short prayer which is prayed in faith and to the point. Elijah on Mount Carmel did not put forth a fancy elaborate prayer, it was just as plain as dirt. 1 Kings 18:36-38 *"And it came to pass at the time of the offering of the evening sacrifice, that Elijah the prophet came near, and said, LORD God of Abraham, Isaac, and of Israel, let it be known this day that thou art God in Israel, and that I am thy servant, and that I have done all these things at thy word. Hear me, O LORD, hear me, that this people may know that thou art the LORD God, and that thou hast turned their heart back again. Then the fire of the LORD fell, and consumed the burnt sacrifice, and the wood, and the stones, and the dust, and licked up the water that was in the trench."* Then God answers the prayer and the chaos is stopped and the world returns to normal and the will of God continues to be done in earth. Matthew 6:9-13 *"After this manner therefore pray ye: Our Father which art in heaven, Hallowed be thy name. Thy kingdom come. Thy will be done in earth, as it is in heaven. Give us this day our daily bread. And forgive us our debts, as we forgive our debtors. And lead us not into temptation, but deliver us from evil: For thine is the kingdom, and the power, and the glory, for ever. Amen."*

It was not a free ride but required them to pour the oil into every vessel. They had to find buyers and then carry the oil to the customers and get paid. Once the empty vessels ran out, then there was no more oil to pour. To everything there is a season. We need to pray for wisdom on how to work during our current season. The season may change and with the change of season will come a new calling and ministry. Let us work hard and realize that we are a tool to be used in the hand of the master.

The Lord also provided more than what was needed to pay the debt. They was able to live on the money left over. God always takes care of His children. If you are faithful to God, He will be faithful to you. We have a promise of a God who will go with us every step of the way. Hebrews 13:5-8 "*Let your conversation be without covetousness; and be content with such things as ye have: for he hath said, I will never leave thee, nor forsake thee. So that we may boldly say, The Lord is my helper, and I will not fear what man shall do unto me. Remember them which have the rule over you, who have spoken unto you the word of God: whose faith follow, considering the end of their conversation. Jesus Christ the same yesterday, and to day, and for ever.*"

Discussion Questions

1. What does God want from us?

____

____

____

2. What has the fear of the Lord brought in your life?

____

____

____

3. Why did the widow need to borrow vessels?

____

____

____

4. What does God want you to give?

____

____

____

5. What type of prayer will work a miracle?

____

____

____

DOUBLE PORTION
The Miracles Of Elisha

Lesson Six

Birth And Death

The cycle of life continues on. New babies are born and the elderly pass on to their reward. Somewhere in between these two metamorphic events we come face to face with the grace of God. Titus 2:11-13 *"For the grace of God that bringeth salvation hath appeared to all men, Teaching us that, denying ungodliness and worldly lusts, we should live soberly, righteously, and godly, in this present world; Looking for that blessed hope, and the glorious appearing of the great God and our Saviour Jesus Christ."* I call this our God moment. If we respond to this call from God and repent we can begin to live a life of purpose and fulfillment. These moment when man responds to the call of the Almighty is what the church is commissioned to facilitate. Sometimes these moments happen close to the birth end of the timeline. But if they do not happen before the death end, it is too late. After death the books are closed and nothing can be added. It is these books they will be opened on judgement day and mankind will be judged according to his works. Revelation 20:12-15 *"And I saw the dead, small and great, stand before God; and the books were opened: and another book was opened, which is the book of life: and the dead were judged out of those things which were written in the books, according to their works. And the sea gave up the dead which were in it; and death and hell delivered up the dead which were in them: and they were judged every man according to their works. And death and hell were cast into the lake of fire. This is the second death. And whosoever was not found written in the book of life was cast into the lake of fire."*

In today's lesson we find birth and death colliding with the will of God. In the end when the laws of nature collide with the will of God they lose. We serve a God who has all power in heaven and in earth. There is nothing that can stop God. When God says it is going to happen, get ready for the whole world to shift to comply with the will of God. Through the Prophet Micah, God said that the Messiah would be born in Bethlehem. Micah 5:2 *"But thou, Bethlehem Ephratah, though thou be little among the thousands of Judah, yet out of thee shall he come forth unto me that is to be ruler in Israel; whose goings forth have been from of old, from everlasting."* So when it came time for the Messiah to be born and Mary was in Nazareth, something had to give. Luke 2:1-7 *"And it came to pass in those days, that there went out a decree from Caesar Augustus, that all the world should be taxed. (And this taxing was first made when Cyrenius was governor of Syria.) And all went to be taxed, every one into his own city. And Joseph also went up from Galilee, out of the city of Nazareth, into Judaea, unto the city of David, which is called Bethlehem; (because he was of the house and lineage of David:) To be taxed with Mary his espoused wife, being great with child. And so it was, that, while they were there, the days were accomplished that she should be delivered. And she brought forth her firstborn son, and wrapped him in swaddling clothes, and laid him in a manger; because there was no room for them in the inn."* Do you see what just happen here? God moves upon the ruler of the civilized world and cause him to impose a tax on the whole world so that Jesus was born in Bethlehem. This means thousands of people are moved around the globe so that one person would be in the right place at the right time. God will upset the whole known universe to keep his promises.

Scripture Text

2 Kings 4:8-37 *"And it fell on a day, that Elisha passed to Shunem, where was a great woman; and she constrained him to eat bread. And so it was, that as oft as he passed by, he turned in thither to eat bread. 9 And she said unto her husband, Behold now, I perceive that this is an holy man of God, which passeth by*

us continually. 10 Let us make a little chamber, I pray thee, on the wall; and let us set for him there a bed, and a table, and a stool, and a candlestick: and it shall be, when he cometh to us, that he shall turn in thither. 11 And it fell on a day, that he came thither, and he turned into the chamber, and lay there. 12 And he said to Gehazi his servant, Call this Shunammite. And when he had called her, she stood before him. 13 And he said unto him, Say now unto her, Behold, thou hast been careful for us with all this care; what is to be done for thee? wouldest thou be spoken for to the king, or to the captain of the host? And she answered, I dwell among mine own people. 14 And he said, What then is to be done for her? And Gehazi answered, Verily she hath no child, and her husband is old. 15 And he said, Call her. And when he had called her, she stood in the door. 16 And he said, About this season, according to the time of life, thou shalt embrace a son. And she said, Nay, my lord, thou man of God, do not lie unto thine handmaid. 17 And the woman conceived, and bare a son at that season that Elisha had said unto her, according to the time of life. 18 And when the child was grown, it fell on a day, that he went out to his father to the reapers. 19 And he said unto his father, My head, my head. And he said to a lad, Carry him to his mother. 20 And when he had taken him, and brought him to his mother, he sat on her knees till noon, and then died. 21 And she went up, and laid him on the bed of the man of God, and shut the door upon him, and went out. 22 And she called unto her husband, and said, Send me, I pray thee, one of the young men, and one of the asses, that I may run to the man of God, and come again. 23 And he said, Wherefore wilt thou go to him to day? it is neither new moon, nor sabbath. And she said, It shall be well. 24 Then she saddled an ass, and said to her servant, Drive, and go forward; slack not thy riding for me, except I bid thee. 25 So she went and came unto the man of God to mount Carmel. And it came to pass, when the man of God saw her afar off, that he said to Gehazi his servant, Behold, yonder is that Shunammite: 26 Run now, I pray thee, to meet her, and say unto her, Is it well with thee? is it well with thy husband? is it well with the child? And she answered, It is well. 27 And when she came to the man of God to the hill, she caught him by the feet: but Gehazi came near to thrust her away. And the man of God said, Let her alone; for her soul is vexed within her: and the LORD hath hid it from me, and hath not told me. 28 Then she said, Did I desire a son of my lord? did I not say, Do not deceive me? 29 Then he said to Gehazi, Gird up thy loins, and take my staff in thine hand, and go thy way: if thou meet any man, salute him not; and if any salute thee, answer him not again: and lay my staff upon the face of the child. 30 And the mother of the child said, As the LORD liveth, and as thy soul liveth, I will not leave thee. And he arose, and followed her. 31 And Gehazi passed on before them, and laid the staff upon the face of the child; but there was neither voice, nor hearing. Wherefore he went again to meet him, and told him, saying, The child is not awaked. 32 And when Elisha was come into the house, behold, the child was dead, and laid upon his bed. 33 He went in therefore, and shut the door upon them twain, and prayed unto the LORD. 34 And he went up, and lay upon the child, and put his mouth upon his mouth, and his eyes upon his eyes, and his hands upon his hands: and he stretched himself upon the child; and the flesh of the child waxed warm. 35 Then he returned, and walked in the house to and fro; and went up, and stretched himself upon him: and the child sneezed seven times, and the child opened his eyes. 36 And he called Gehazi, and said, Call this Shunammite. So he called her. And when she was come in unto him, he said, Take up thy son. 37 Then she went in, and fell at his feet, and bowed herself to the ground, and took up her son, and went out."

The Great Woman

2 Kings 4:8 "And it fell on a day, that Elisha passed to Shunem, where was a great woman; and she constrained him to eat bread. And so it was, that as oft as he passed by, he turned in thither to eat bread.

The great woman who was the recipient of this miracle resided at Shunem, which appears to mean "uneven." Shunem is mentioned only twice elsewhere in the Old Testament. In Joshua 19:18 it is described as a territory allotted to the tribe of Issachar. In 1 Samuel 28:4 we are told it was the place that the Philistines gathered themselves together and pitched in battle array against Israel. It seems that Shunem was on the road between Samaria and Mount Carmel, a road which Elisha traveled to visit the different Schools of the Prophets. It appeared to be a farming district and in this charming country life we find the clash of birth and death.

The Hebrew word "gadol" (<u>great</u>) is used in various Bible verses with slightly different meanings. In Genesis 1:16, 21 and several other passages it refers to material or physical greatness. In 2 Kings 5:1, Proverbs 25:6 and Job 1:3 it is associated with social prominence. This great woman had material possessions and money, as is illustrated by the servants they had and their buildings and their ability to provide a private room for the prophet. There are those who have been blessed with great material possession who fear and serve the Lord. This woman was also <u>great</u> spiritually. She was <u>great</u> in hospitality. She also perceived that Elisha was a holy man of God. She had wisdom to discern that Elisha would desire rest and privacy.

Elisha seemed to have a circuit through the land in order to visit the Schools of the Prophets and to instruct the people. At first Elisha refused her hospitality. Several important points are advocated by this. A minister should not be presumptuous by pressing himself upon people. A minister should always wait until he is invited to be a part of something. A Minister is not required to spend all his days living in a cave or sojourning by a brook like Elijah. God will always provide us with someone to bless us. Jesus had moments when there was no place to lay his head yet there were many women who ministered unto him of their substance (Luke 8:2-3). The apostle Paul made tents to provide for his needs, yet the saints loved and esteemed him highly for his work's sake. Elisha experienced hardship while he was with Elijah but now was being blessed with hospitality. Hospitality is required of the saints. Romans 12:9-13 *"Let love be without dissimulation. Abhor that which is evil; cleave to that which is good. Be kindly affectioned one to another with brotherly love; in honour preferring one another; Not slothful in business; fervent in spirit; serving the Lord; Rejoicing in hope; patient in tribulation; continuing instant in prayer; Distributing to the necessity of saints; given to hospitality."* The ministry is also required to be given to hospitality (Titus 1:8), and that without grudging (1 Peter 4:9). This great woman took the initiative and did not wait until asked by Elisha. She was on the lookout for him and always found a way to bless the man of God.

A Room For The Prophet

> 2 Kings 4:9-10 And she said unto her husband, Behold now, I perceive that this is an holy man of God, which passeth by us continually. 10 Let us make a little chamber, I pray thee, on the wall; and let us set for him there a bed, and a table, and a stool, and a candlestick: and it shall be, when he cometh to us, that he shall turn in thither.

Apparently she was the owner of this property, for her husband is not called a great man. Yet we find her talking with him and seeking his input. Thereby she leaves her sisters everywhere a marvelous example. Ephesians 5:21-25 "*Submitting yourselves one to another in the fear of God. Wives, submit yourselves unto your own husbands, as unto the Lord. For the husband is the head of the wife, even as Christ is the head of the church: and he is the saviour of the body. Therefore as the church is subject unto Christ, so let the wives be to their own husbands in every thing. Husbands, love your wives, even as Christ also loved the church, and gave himself for it.*" How much domestic conflict could be avoided if there was more of this mutual discussing? But we must also realize that Ephesians 5 does not give the husband the right to demand his wife to disobey God. Acts 5:29 "*Then Peter and the other apostles answered and said, We ought to obey God rather than men.*"

This great woman of Shunem was gifted with spiritual discernment, for she perceived that Elisha was a holy man of God. It is those who walk in truth and are subject to spiritual authority (Pastor) who are granted spiritual discernment. 1 Corinthians 2:12-15 "*Now we have received, not the spirit of the world, but the spirit which is of God; that we might know the things that are freely given to us of God. Which things also we speak, not in the words which man's wisdom teacheth, but which the Holy Ghost teacheth; comparing spiritual things with spiritual. But the natural man receiveth not the things of the Spirit of God: for they are foolishness unto him: neither can he know them, because they are spiritually discerned. But he that is spiritual judgeth all things, yet he himself is judged of no man.*" It is when we forsake the path of obedience that our judgment is marred (Jeremiah 18:4) and our perception perverted. Psalms 119:97-100 "*O how love I thy law! it is my meditation all the day. Thou through thy commandments hast made me wiser than mine enemies: for they are ever with me. I have more understanding than all my teachers: for thy testimonies are my meditation. I understand more than the ancients, because I keep thy precepts."*

Gehazi Appears On The Scene

> 2 Kings 4:11-12 *"And it fell on a day, that he came thither, and he turned into the chamber, and lay there. 12 And he said to Gehazi his servant, Call this Shunammite. And when he had called her, she stood before him."*

The fact that Gehazi is traveling with Elisha and is carrying messages to other people for Elisha would cause us to believe that Elisha is starting to groom Gehazi to be a great prophet as Elijah had groomed him. In lesson nine we will take an in-depth look at the servant Gehazi. Oh what a glorious opportunity it is to be brought on the ministry team and get to work with the anointed men of God. Remember you are there to learn, they did not bring you aboard because they need instruction. So keep your opinions to yourself and do it like they tell you to do it. As a young minister do everything you can to be able to be with and observe your Pastor as he does the work of God. Sometimes it may be as simple as carrying his iPad Bible (I can remember the good old days when it was a leather bound book) and opening doors for him but what you will learn cannot be bought with a price.

Returning The Blessing

> 2 Kings 4:13-14 *"And he said unto him, Say now unto her, Behold, thou hast been careful for us with all this care; what is to be done for thee? wouldest thou be spoken for to the king, or to the captain of the host? 14 And she answered, I dwell among mine own people. And he said, What then is to be done for her? And Gehazi answered, Verily she hath no child, and her husband is old."*

It was not with complacency that Elisha accepted the loving hospitality of the great woman as though it was something due him because of his position. His actions proved he was truly grateful and wanted to show his appreciation. There are many who call themselves ministers today who have a proud attitude and demand that everyone treats them like a god. But a true man of God always walks in humility. So Elisha begin to look for a way to bless the great woman with something more than his service to God. Most of the time it was people asking Elisha for help in their time of distress but this time Elisha went looking for the need. The Lord has blessed Elisha and he now had a working relationship with King Jehoram of Israel (2 Kings 3:1-27). So he was willing to share the blessing that the Lord has given him, the ear of the king. We are blessed to be a blessing. Many times people lose their blessing because they do not realize that we are blessed so that we can bless other. When we hoard the blessing to ourselves we will lose them. The great woman was content with her material possession and her position in life. 1 Timothy 6:3-10 *"If any man teach otherwise, and consent not to wholesome words, even the words of our Lord Jesus Christ, and to the doctrine which is according to godliness; He is proud, knowing nothing, but doting about questions and strifes of words, whereof cometh envy, strife, railings, evil surmisings, Perverse disputings of men of corrupt minds, and destitute of the truth, supposing that gain is godliness: from such withdraw thyself. But godliness with contentment is great gain. For we brought nothing into this world, and it is certain we can carry nothing out. And having food and raiment let us be therewith content. But they that will be rich fall into temptation and a snare, and into many foolish and hurtful lusts, which drown men in destruction and perdition. For the love of money is the root of all evil: which while some coveted after, they have erred from the faith, and pierced themselves through with many sorrows."*

Gehazi showed his potential to become a great prophet. Gehazi perceived the thing that was lacking in her life was a child. Childlessness was a tragedy for a woman in Israel and the barren wife was likely to be reviled by her husband, family and society at large. There are many childless couples in the church today and they need our prayers and support. Some holidays are very difficult for them, so let us handle them with care. A childless couple should never become bitter and blame God or lash out at others because of their hurt. Check your spirit and get involved in helping children who are in need of loving care.

God's Favor and Reward

2 Kings 4:15-17 *"And he said, Call her. And when he had called her, she stood in the door. 16 And he said, About this season, according to the time of life, thou shalt embrace a son. And she said, Nay, my lord, thou man of God, do not lie unto thine handmaid. 17 And the woman conceived, and bare a son at that season that Elisha had said unto her, according to the time of life."*

Several times in the Old Testament the miraculous birth of a son was the results of God's favor being displayed in their life. We see that in the lives of Abraham, Isaac, Hannah, Manoah and now this great woman. Matthew 10:41 *"He that receiveth a prophet in the name of a prophet shall receive a prophet's reward; and he that receiveth a righteous man in the name of a righteous man shall receive a righteous man's reward."* This great woman had honored and blessed Elisha in a day when prophets were far from being popular. You have a Pastor that preaches the truth and the truth is not always popular. But the truth is the most valuable thing in our world today. Matthew 13:44 *"Again, the kingdom of heaven is like unto treasure hid in a field; the which when a man hath found, he hideth, and for joy thereof goeth and selleth all that he hath, and buyeth that field."* The truth is that you must be born again to enter the Kingdom of God (John 3:1-8). Don't trade the truth for popularity.

There are times in our lives when we think we want something and God does not give it to us. But if we will be thankful for what he does give us the day will come when He will bless us with something we never imagined that we could have. This great woman had given up on the ideal of having a son and was just thankful for God's blessing even though she greatly desired one. Did Joseph ever give up on his dreams? How can you imagine being a ruler when you are put in a dungeon for the rest of your life? Not only will God give you favor but he will also reward you. Don't ever give up on a dream or calling that God gives you.

In The Hour Of Tragedy

2 Kings 4:18-22 *"And when the child was grown, it fell on a day, that he went out to his father to the reapers. 19 And he said unto his father, My head, my head. And he said to a lad, Carry him to his mother. 20 And when he had taken him, and brought him to his mother, he sat on her knees till noon, and then died. 21 And she went up, and laid him on the bed of the man of God, and shut the door upon him, and went out. 22 And she called unto her husband, and said, Send me, I pray thee, one of the young men, and one of the asses, that I may run to the man of God, and come again."*

After the birth of the son, Elisha was now more than just a guest in the home, he was now loved like family. I am sure the great woman was looking for more ways to make his life comfortable. As the son grew the influence of the prophet help bring up the boy in the fear of God. This was the miracle child from the Lord and just like the Prophet Samuel the mother would want him to serve the Lord. If we will take our children to church so that they can be taught the Word of God and live it before them at home they will forever remember the right way. Proverbs 22:6 *"Train up a child in the way he should go: and when he is old, he will not depart from it."*

Then suddenly the tragedy strikes and the boy becomes ill. It seems the father did not suspect anything serious. The father sent the boy back home with one of his younger workers. We never know what tomorrow will bring but we know who holds tomorrow in His hand. The boy will greatly loved by his mother and she took him in her arms and comforted him. We live in a sad day, thousands of mothers are deserting their children to go live the life of a party girl. How sad it will be for those mothers when they are old because their children will not acknowledge them. While the boy is in his mother's arm his life leaves him. The day had started out so happy, the son going to work with his father and by noon he was lying dead on the bed of the prophet. Life will sometimes blindside us with tragedy. Our hopes and dreams seem to be destroyed before our eyes in the tick of one heartbeat. How could it be that the wonderful gift that God had given them was taken away so soon?

Once again her spiritual greatness shines forth. There was no paralyzing despair, no stampede of grief. She did not blame God foolishly. Job 1:20-22 *"Then Job arose, and rent his mantle, and shaved his head, and fell down upon the ground, and worshipped, And said, Naked came I out of my mother's womb, and naked shall I return thither: the LORD gave, and the LORD hath taken away; blessed be the name of the LORD. In all this Job sinned not, nor charged God foolishly."* Her action of placing her dead son on the bed of the prophet shows her faith in the man of God.

Knowing Where To Go

2 Kings 4:23-26 *"And he said, Wherefore wilt thou go to him to day? it is neither new moon, nor sabbath. And she said, It shall be well. 24 Then she saddled an ass, and said to her servant, Drive, and go forward; slack not thy riding for me, except I bid thee. 25 So she went and came unto the man of God to mount Carmel. And it came to pass, when the man of God saw her afar off, that he said to Gehazi his servant, Behold, yonder is that Shunammite: 26 Run now, I pray thee, to meet her, and say unto her, Is it well with thee? is it well with thy husband? is it well with the child? And she answered, It is well."*

This was an urgent situation but she still took time to inform her husband where she was going. Once again, open communication is displayed in this marriage. Her husband during this tragedy had no idea where to go. If it had been a church night he would have known where the prophet was because they were faithful to the house of God. The great woman had paid more attention to the prophet schedule and knew that he was teaching at the School of the Prophets at Mount Carmel that day. It was a long hard journey from Shunem to Mount Carmel but she was determined to get to the man of God. Mark 5:25-34 *"And a certain woman, which had an issue of blood twelve years, And had suffered many things of many physicians, and had spent all that she had, and was nothing bettered, but rather grew worse, When she had heard of Jesus, came in the press behind, and touched his garment. For she said, If I may touch but his clothes, I shall be whole. And straightway the fountain of her blood was dried up; and she felt in her body that she was healed of that plague. And Jesus, immediately knowing in himself that virtue had gone out of him, turned him about in the press, and said, Who touched my clothes? And his disciples said unto him, Thou seest the multitude thronging thee, and sayest thou, Who touched me? And he looked round about to see her that had done this thing. But the woman fearing and trembling, knowing what was done in her, came and fell down before him, and told him all the truth. And he said unto her, Daughter, thy faith hath made thee whole; go in peace, and be whole of thy plague."* Many times we are tempted to stay home from church when problems come our way. Staying home from church will only make the problem worst, we need to touch Jesus as soon as we can when problems come our way.

Elisha was working on training Gehazi on how to have compassion for people. So he send him to meet the great woman and find out what her destress was. We have examples of Paul using young minister to do task for him so that he might spend more time doing the work of the Lord. 2 Timothy 4:11-13 *"Only Luke is with me. Take Mark, and bring him with thee: for he is profitable to me for the ministry. And Tychicus have I sent to Ephesus. The cloke that I left at Troas with Carpus, when thou comest, bring with thee, and the books, but especially the parchments."* Sometimes the Lord will reveal our problems to the man of God. Most of the time the Lord wants us to go to the man of God and tell him about our problems so that he may help us.

The Warning Bells Begin To Ring

2 Kings 4:27-31 *"And when she came to the man of God to the hill, she caught him by the feet: but Gehazi came near to thrust her away. And the man of God said, Let her alone; for her soul is vexed within her: and the LORD hath hid it from me, and hath not told me. 28 Then she said, Did I desire a son of my lord? did I not say, Do not deceive me? 29 Then he said to Gehazi, Gird up thy loins, and*

take my staff in thine hand, and go thy way: if thou meet any man, salute him not; and if any salute thee, answer him not again: and lay my staff upon the face of the child. 30 And the mother of the child said, As the LORD liveth, and as thy soul liveth, I will not leave thee. And he arose, and followed her. 31 And Gehazi passed on before them, and laid the staff upon the face of the child; but there was neither voice, nor hearing. Wherefore he went again to meet him, and told him, saying, The child is not awaked."

Gehazi shows an utter lack of compassion here and starts to remove the great woman from the room because of her grief. Elisha at this point does not even know what the problems was and Gehazi is being rude and calloused. The great woman pours out her pain and grief to the man of God and reminds him of her request to him before the son was born. At this point rather than throwing Gehazi in the trash heap, Elisha gives him another chance to prove his faith to God and loyalty to him. 1 Timothy 3:6-7 *"Not a novice, lest being lifted up with pride he fall into the condemnation of the devil. Moreover he must have a good report of them which are without; lest he fall into reproach and the snare of the devil."* By giving the staff to Gehazi he is authorizing him to go under his anointing and perform a miracle. This was a very urgent and important mission that Elisha was sending Gehazi on. He gave very specific instructions to Gehazi upon what he must do, just like the specific instruction he had given the widow woman in the previous lesson. When the widow woman followed his instructions the miracle happen. Rather than staying with the boy and praying until the prophet arrives, he lays the staff on him and then jumps up and returns to the prophet to tell him that his idea had not worked. He doesn't even pray over the boy. Bing, bong the bells ring, as the carnal so called saints pop in and out of the altars like popcorn, if they even go and pray after the preaching. When you hear the preaching of the Word of God you need to respond. The failure was not in the faith of Elisha but was a failure in the faith of Gehazi.

The Prayer Of A Righteous Man

2 Kings 4:32-37 "And when Elisha was come into the house, behold, the child was dead, and laid upon his bed. 33 He went in therefore, and shut the door upon them twain, and prayed unto the LORD. 34 And he went up, and lay upon the child, and put his mouth upon his mouth, and his eyes upon his eyes, and his hands upon his hands: and he stretched himself upon the child; and the flesh of the child waxed warm. 35 Then he returned, and walked in the house to and fro; and went up, and stretched himself upon him: and the child sneezed seven times, and the child opened his eyes. 36 And he called Gehazi, and said, Call this Shunammite. So he called her. And when she was come in unto him, he said, Take up thy son. 37 Then she went in, and fell at his feet, and bowed herself to the ground, and took up her son, and went out."

Just as Elisha had commanded the widow woman to shut the door, he goes into the room and shuts the door. Matthew 6:1-6 *"Take heed that ye do not your alms before men, to be seen of them: otherwise ye have no reward of your Father which is in heaven. Therefore when thou doest thine alms, do not sound a trumpet before thee, as the hypocrites do in the synagogues and in the streets, that they may have glory of men. Verily I say unto you, They have their reward. But when thou doest alms, let not thy left hand know what thy right hand doeth: That thine alms may be in secret: and thy Father which seeth in secret himself shall reward thee openly. And when thou prayest, thou shalt not be as the hypocrites are: for they love to pray standing in the synagogues and in the corners of the streets, that they may be seen of men. Verily I say unto you, They have their reward. But thou, when thou prayest, enter into thy closet, and when thou hast shut thy door, pray to thy Father which is in secret; and thy Father which seeth in secret shall reward thee openly."* Now was the time for the man of God to touch heaven with his prayers. We need to learn what it means to pray until we touch heaven. The disciples had not learned that yet in the garden of Gethsemane.

The actions of Elisha are the same as the prophet Elijah. 1 Kings 17:17-22 *"And it came to pass after these things, that the son of the woman, the mistress of the house, fell sick; and his sickness was so sore, that there was no breath left in him. And she said unto Elijah, What have I to do with thee, O thou man of God? art thou come unto me to call my sin to remembrance, and to slay my son? And he said unto her, Give me thy son. And he took him out of her bosom, and carried him up into a loft, where he abode, and laid him upon his own bed. And he cried unto the LORD, and said, O LORD my God, hast thou also brought evil upon the widow with whom I sojourn, by slaying her son? And he stretched himself upon the child three times, and cried unto the LORD, and said, O LORD my God, I pray thee, let this child's soul come into him again. And the LORD heard the voice of Elijah; and the soul of the child came into him again, and he revived."* We are to never forsake the old landmarks. It is those proven things of God that we are to fall back on in the time of need. When David went to fight the giant, he refused to put on Saul's armor because it was not proven. There is no weapon in the universe that can compare to the power of prayer. James 5:13-16 *"Is any among you afflicted? let him pray. Is any merry? let him sing psalms. Is any sick among you? let him call for the elders of the church; and let them pray over him, anointing him with oil in the name of the Lord: And the prayer of faith shall save the sick, and the Lord shall raise him up; and if he have committed sins, they shall be forgiven him. Confess your faults one to another, and pray one for another, that ye may be healed. The effectual fervent prayer of a righteous man availeth much."* Our God is still in the healing business today. It does not matter how hopeless our case may seem, we serve a God who has all power in heaven and in earth. Neither birth nor death escapes the power of Jesus. Just like God raised up the great woman son, God healing virtue is still flowing in the church today.

Discussion Questions

1.   What does grace teach us?

____

____

____

2.   How did the great woman bless Elisha?

____

____

____

3.   How do we receive a prophet's reward?

____

____

____

4.   Where do we need to go in the time of trouble?

____

____

____

5.   Why did Elisha stretched himself upon the child?

____

____

____

Lesson Seven

Deliverance From Another Quarter

When it comes to the working of the Lord we need to learn how to think outside the box. Many times the only avenues we are willing to explore are the ones we have traveled before. It is very easy to get stuck in a rut and the old carnal man is definitely a creature of habit. The old carnal man had always depended upon the flesh to provide for him. We now realize that it is useless to go back to those empty wells of carnal pleasure to find fulfillment and purpose in life. 2 Timothy 3:1-7 *"This know also, that in the last days perilous times shall come. For men shall be lovers of their own selves, covetous, boasters, proud, blasphemers, disobedient to parents, unthankful, unholy, Without natural affection, trucebreakers, false accusers, incontinent, fierce, despisers of those that are good, Traitors, heady, highminded, lovers of pleasures more than lovers of God; Having a form of godliness, but denying the power thereof: from such turn away. For of this sort are they which creep into houses, and lead captive silly women laden with sins, led away with divers lusts, Ever learning, and never able to come to the knowledge of the truth."* But when one begins to follow Jesus he begins to walk down some new paths. The path of faith is a totally new concept to a new believer. To be able to trust God and put your life in His hands is a very big step. In the past we depended upon what we could see with our carnal eyes. Even in our walk with Christ it is easy to get comfortable with just the paths we are familiar with and never accept the idea that God can provide deliverance from another quarter. We get comfortable with God paying the church bills with the money from the offering plate and begin to panic when the offering plate is short. God has also paid the church bills by sending a check in the mail, by placing money in the gutter in front of the church, by using an unclean bird (1 Kings 17:6) to hand you money, by putting money into the checking account, by giving you a bonus on the job, by having someone else pay the bill to the vendor and by having the vendor cancel the bill etc.. If you have never experienced God providing by these other methods then it is hard to believe it will happen when the offering plate is short. We do not have God in a box and do not control how he will provide. But we know that what God mandates, he will provide a way to make it happen.

At one time the prophets at the Schools of the Prophets were feed by Obadiah. I am sure that the prophets had gotten used to having food without having to worry about where it was coming from. Now Obadiah is gone on to his reward and no longer able to feed them. We serve an on time God. Just because Obadiah was no longer providing food did not mean that God was done with the Schools of the Prophets. Yes it was nip and tuck for a few days but God always comes through. When one door is shut, God always opens a window. Hebrews 13:5-8 *"Let your conversation be without covetousness; and be content with such things as ye have: for he hath said, I will never leave thee, nor forsake thee. So that we may boldly say, The Lord is my helper, and I will not fear what man shall do unto me. Remember them which have the rule over you, who have spoken unto you the word of God: whose faith follow, considering the end of their conversation. Jesus Christ the same yesterday, and to day, and for ever."* If God can use Elisha to help feed the prophets, he can use your Pastor to lead you through these last days.

Scripture Text

2 Kings 4:38-44 *"And Elisha came again to Gilgal: and there was a dearth in the land; and the sons of the prophets were sitting before him: and he said unto his servant, Set on the great pot, and see the pottage for the sons of the prophets. 39 And one went out into the field to gather herbs, and found a wild vine, and*

gathered thereof wild gourds his lap full, and came and shred them into the pot of pottage: for they knew them not. 40 So they poured out for the men to eat. And it came to pass, as they were eating of the pottage, that they cried out, and said, O thou man of God, there is death in the pot. And they could not eat thereof. 41 But he said, Then bring meal. And he cast it into the pot; and he said, Pour out for the people, that they may eat. And there was no harm in the pot. 42 And there came a man from Baalshalisha, and brought the man of God bread of the firstfruits, twenty loaves of barley, and full ears of corn in the husk thereof. And he said, Give unto the people, that they may eat. 43 And his servitor said, What, should I set this before an hundred men? He said again, Give the people, that they may eat: for thus saith the LORD, They shall eat, and shall leave thereof. 44 So he set it before them, and they did eat, and left thereof, according to the word of the LORD."

The Setting

Gilgal was close to the Jordan River and to the east of Jericho. It was a region that had more moisture and vegetation than the areas further from the Jordan River. It was at Gilgal that the nation of Israel had set up twelve stones as a monument to God's safe passage through the Jordan River on dry ground while the armies of Egypt drown. The miraculous supply of manna had ceased when the nation of Israel had got to Gilgal because they begin to eat of the bounty of the land (Joshua 5:11-12). Many wonderful things had happen at Gilgal but now they were suffering with the rest of the nation because wickedness was on every hand. Famine is one of the four sore judgements which the Lord promises to the people who forsake Him for other Gods. Ezekiel 14:21 *"For thus saith the Lord GOD; How much more when I send my four sore judgments upon Jerusalem, the sword, and the famine, and the noisome beast, and the pestilence, to cut off from it man and beast?"* How will America escape the judgements of God? Wickedness and perversion has been promoted and applauded unchecked in our land. For several years now we have been a nation with a famine. It is not a famine of bread and water but a famine of people refusing to hear the Word of the Lord (Amos 8:11). The modern day church has become entertainment centers, social clubs and concert halls. Sin is no longer being preached against in their pulpits. America has allowed a pestilent to shut the doors of their churches while anarchy runs free in the streets.   It is time for the message of repentance, baptism in the name of Jesus, and Holy Ghost infilling be proclaimed across our land. We are looking for God to bring us deliverance from another quarter so that we may freely proclaim the truth to a lost and miserable nation. Let the light of the true church shine bright and truth be proclaimed on every corner.

Soul Food

> 2 Kings 4:38 *"And Elisha came again to Gilgal: and there was a dearth in the land; and the sons of the prophets were sitting before him: and he said unto his servant, Set on the great pot, and see the pottage for the sons of the prophets."*

Once again we find Elisha at the School of the Prophets in Gilgal giving them instructions on the things of God as they set before him. The prophets sitting before Elisha showed their respect and a desire to learn. This reminds us of Mary who sat at Jesus' feet so she could hear the Word of Lord, which Jesus emphasized as the good part and the thing that was needful (Luke 10:39-42). There was a great famine in the land, so food was not easy to come by in Gilgal. At the end of his teaching session, he ask his servant to put on the great pot and begin to prepare a meal for the students. The Hebrew word rendered "servitor" in this passage is elsewhere rendered "minister," "servant" (Exodus 24:13, 33:11) referring to Joshua the successor of Moses. From the text of the previous passages this servitor would have been Gehazi. Once again proof that Elisha was grooming Gehazi to succeed him as the next prophet of Israel. Just as Jesus was concerned about the spiritual matters first, He did not forget that people had need of nourishment too.   Matthew 6:31-33 *"Therefore take no thought, saying, What shall we eat? or, What shall we drink? or, Wherewithal shall we be clothed? (For after all these things do the Gentiles seek:) for your heavenly Father knoweth that ye have need of all these things. But seek ye first the kingdom of God, and his righteousness; and all these things shall be added unto you."*   So after the teaching, Elisha called for a meal to be prepared.

The Loose Cannon

> 2 Kings 4:39 *" And one went out into the field to gather*

herbs, and found a wild vine, and gathered thereof wild gourds his lap full, and came and shred them into the pot of pottage: for they knew them not."

Without being ask, one of the young prophets goes out into the fields to gathers plants for the pot. He finds a wild vine and begins to gather the fruit thereof. There are many things that need to be done in the church. We first need to inquire of the Pastor how he wants them done and when he wants them done. After we are given instruction on the way to conduct the work of the Lord decently and in order, we need to do the work of our calling without being poke and prodded. 1 Corinthians 14:40 *"Let all things be done decently and in order."* It is obvious that this young prophet is a novice and does not know everything that he needed to know in order to gather wholesome plants. While zeal is a wonderful thing it is a lot like fire. When fire is contained and regulated it provides many wonderful benefits to mankind. It is fire burning in a gas heater that keeps us warm in the winter. It is fire burning to make steam that makes electricity to light our lights and run our computers. It is when we see fire burning without containment and guidelines like a forest fire that we see great damage. So allow that zeal to be channeled into service that is productive for the Kingdom of God. They are some things which get lots of attention and produce excitement but in the long run do not further the Kingdom of God.

Poisons Of The Body and Spirit

2 Kings 4:40 *"So they poured out for the men to eat. And it came to pass, as they were eating of the pottage, that they cried out, and said, O thou man of God, there is death in the pot. And they could not eat thereof."*

The young prophet picked a great deal of the wild gourds and carried them back to the school and cut them up and put them into the pot. There is no evidence to suggest that he knew that the plant were poisonous. It was not until the pottage was served that the poisonous plant was identified. It was the students who had been sitting at the feet of Elisha who now discovered the poison that was put in the pot. This passage is given to us to help us learn about spiritual discernment also. It is those who are instructed by a Godly Pastor who will begin to build spiritual discernment and better judgment about the things of the spirit world.   Mark 4:21-24 *"And he said unto them, Is a candle brought to be put under a bushel, or under a bed? and not to be set on a candlestick? For there is nothing hid, which shall not be manifested; neither was any thing kept secret, but that it should come abroad. If any man have ears to hear, let him hear. And he said unto them, Take heed what ye hear: with what measure ye mete, it shall be measured to you: and unto you that hear shall more be given."* Don't get your spiritual food from the fast food hirelings.

Sometimes we forget that we are surrounded by potential death at all times. The curse of sin brought poison into our world because of Adam and Eve. Romans 8:22-23 *"For we know that the whole creation groaneth and travaileth in pain together until now. And not only they, but ourselves also, which have the firstfruits of the Spirit, even we ourselves groan within ourselves, waiting for the adoption, to wit, the redemption of our body."* Just because we have the Holy Ghost does not exempt us from the pains of life. It is not until we get to heaven that we will find complete deliverance from the curse of sin. The most innocent looking plant or berry can produce the most painful suffering or death to man. Everywhere we look, we can see how sin is corrupting all areas of our world today. Revelation 21:1-4 *"And I saw a new heaven and a new earth: for the first heaven and the first earth were passed away; and there was no more sea. And I John saw the holy city, new Jerusalem, coming down from God out of heaven, prepared as a bride adorned for her husband. And I heard a great voice out of heaven saying, Behold, the tabernacle of God is with men, and he will dwell with them, and they shall be his people, and God himself shall be with them, and be their God. And God shall wipe away all tears from their eyes; and there shall be no more death, neither sorrow, nor crying, neither shall there be any more pain: for the former things are passed away."* Heaven is the only place that will be free from all sin. This earth will never become a paradise. While upon this earth we must be careful to not partake of the poisons of the flesh and spirit.

The things that poison our spiritual man are so very subtle in this day and time. We have a religious system today that is more about providing wealth and power for its leaders than providing truth and hope to the lost and wayward. We have a climate where church goers are looking for soothing words that will show them the way to prosperity and immortality on this earth. While these words are sweet to the ear they bring poison into the soul that will slowing remove man from the presence of God. 2 Timothy 2:15-17 *"Study to shew thyself approved unto God, a workman that needeth not to be ashamed, rightly dividing the word of truth. But shun profane and vain babblings: for they will increase unto more ungodliness. And their word will eat as doth a canker: of whom is Hymenaeus and Philetus."* We no longer see the religious world studying the Word of God. They take the words of the false prophets which declare they can tell you everything you need to know about salvation in one easy step; Believe on Jesus as your personal Savior. Then they tell them it is now time for you to make Jesus your garbage man. Just mess up all you want to and give Him the garbage and He will spin it into gold for you. The Word of God tells us we must repent before God will step in and deliver us out of our pit. If you are living in the pit, then you need to study about repentance. 2 Corinthians 7:10 *"For godly sorrow worketh repentance to salvation not to be repented of: but the sorrow of the world worketh death."*

If we see so much poison spewing out of modern day religion, just imagine how much poison is spewing out of the secular world. 1 Corinthians 2:14 *"But the natural man receiveth not the things of the Spirit of God: for they are foolishness unto him: neither can he know them, because they are spiritually discerned."* The need to put filters in place and shut off every pipeline of poison possible is greater than ever. Everything that we see and hear can have spiritual poison in it. The goal of the enemy is not to suddenly remove us from worshiping the one true God, but to gradually get us involved with others as they worship the gods of this world. Romans 1:25-32 *"Who changed the truth of God into a lie, and worshipped and served the creature more than the Creator, who is blessed for ever. Amen. For this cause God gave them up unto vile affections: for even their women did change the natural use into that which is against nature: And likewise also the men, leaving the natural use of the woman, burned in their lust one toward another; men with men working that which is unseemly, and receiving in themselves that recompence of their error which was meet. And even as they did not like to retain God in their knowledge, God gave them over to a reprobate mind, to do those things which are not convenient; Being filled with all unrighteousness, fornication, wickedness, covetousness, maliciousness; full of envy, murder, debate, deceit, malignity; whisperers, Backbiters, haters of God, despiteful, proud, boasters, inventors of evil things, disobedient to parents, Without understanding, covenantbreakers, without natural affection, implacable, unmerciful: Who knowing the judgment of God, that they which commit such things are worthy of death, not only do the same, but have pleasure in them that do them."*

The Antidote For Poison

> 2 Kings 4:41 *"But he said, Then bring meal. And he cast it Into the pot; and he said, Pour out for the people, that they may eat. And there was no harm in the pot."*

I see the type and shadow of the word "meal" (meal is used to make bread, Isaiah 28:28) here as being the Word of God. John 1:14 *"And the Word was made flesh, and dwelt among us, (and we beheld his glory, the glory as of the only begotten of the Father,) full of grace and truth."* John 6:33-35 *"For the bread of God is he which cometh down from heaven, and giveth life unto the world. Then said they unto him, Lord, evermore give us this bread. And Jesus said unto them, I am the bread of life: he that cometh to me shall never hunger; and he that believeth on me shall never thirst."* Jesus will always use His Word to lead the honest hearts into more truth regardless of the famine of truth that surrounds them. Elisha and the sons of the prophets had meal in the midst of a famine. We can allow nothing to separate us from our Bible, it is the bread of life. Just as someone else fetched the meal, we need the saints of God hiding the Word of God in their hearts and praying for their Pastor so he will have free course to preach the truth. It was Elisha who cast the meal into the pot and we need the preacher to put the Word of God in our pot too. 1 Corinthians 1:21 *"For after that in the wisdom of God the world by wisdom knew not God, it pleased God by the foolishness of preaching to save them that believe."* The ministry must take a stand and preach against sin today. The true church will always have the fivefold ministry teaching and preaching truth in it. Hearing the teaching and preaching of truth in this church is the only antidote to the poison of the deceitfulness of sin.

The working of this miracle once again is at the moment of an urgent need. Elisha is stepping forth to preserve the simple blessing the Lord had already provided. Faith and obedience go hand and hand here to provide an atmosphere to produce the miraculous. The people had to bring what they had, which was meal and then the faith of Elisha propelled him to cast it into the pot and God worked the miracle of removing the harm from the pot. Isaiah 59:19 *"So shall they fear the name of the LORD from the west, and his glory from the rising of the sun. When the enemy shall come in like a flood, the Spirit of the LORD shall lift up a standard against him."* How much faith and obedience did it take for the people then to eat it? Many today would have turned and walked away. How many times do we walk away from our miracle?

Where Did Deliverance Come From?

> 2 Kings 4:42 *"And there came a man from Baalshalisha, and brought the man of God bread of the firstfruits, twenty loaves of barley, and full ears of corn in the husk thereof. And he said, Give unto the people, that they may eat."*

We first see Shalisha mentioned in 1 Samuel 9:4. Now it is called Baalshalisha because the wicked Queen Jezebel had renamed the city by adding the name of her God Baal at the beginning of it as other cities had done (1 Chronicles 5:23). But even in a city which had open promotion of idolatry in it, there was a man who feared God and was willing to hear His voice and obey his commandments. The gates of Hell has never prevailed against the church and they never will. God will always have a people living and preaching the truth. You may be outnumbered and considered peculiar but God will always provide miraculous provisions for his people. We are not given the name of the man who stepped out of Baalshalisha but it is like Moses stepping out of the wilderness, he brings the ingredients for a miracle. Baalshalisha was next to Mount Ephraim and the servant of the Lord undertook a journey of considerable distance in order to bring his tithes unto Elisha. It is obvious that the famine did not extend all the way to Baalshalisha because he had recently harvested barley and corn in the husk to bring to the man of God. He even went the extra mile and baked bread out of some of the barley. Many times it is doing more than that which is required of you which will work the miraculous. Luke 17:10 *"So likewise ye, when ye shall have done all those things which are commanded you, say, We are unprofitable servants: we have done that which was our duty to do."* As a very young minister many years ago I was helping at a youth camp one year. The leader of our group one day got up and ask all the youth to write down a question and put it in the box and that the team would answer them. We got question after question asking about things like; how long does our clothing have to be, how long is long hair, why can't I listen to worldly music, what is wrong with necking, etc.. We did not get one question that day that ask how they could get closer to God. If we spend our time doing just enough to get by, we will never get by. We should not be wanting to see how close to the world we can get, we should be trying to see how close to God we can get. It takes more than just the bare minimums to experience the miraculous. It is going to take men and women of God who are willing to give all they have.

History tells us that Baalshalisha also had the earliest harvest in the land. So what a blessing it was to get an unexpected blessing. If it had come from Samaria or Bethel it would have not been much of a surprise because the Schools of the Prophets there would have been in the habit of sharing their blessings. But this was deliverance from another quarter. It was not expected, but it was direly needed. There is no way that the man from Baalshalisha could have known that what he was bringing was the seeds for a miracle. Many times we could lose our blessings because we get discouraged before we ever start because we sell ourselves short. Allow God to use you to be the catalyst for a miracle in your world. Do something with eternal impact today.

The one passage we find in the Bible that talks about man robbing God is referring to tithes and offering (Malachi 3:8). This man was bringing his tithes (first fruits) to the man of God. Tithing is a principle that was started way before the Law of Moses and was commanded by Jesus. Hebrews 7:1-2 *"For this Melchisedec, king of Salem, priest of the most high God, who met Abraham returning from the slaughter of the kings, and blessed him; To whom also Abraham gave a tenth part of all; first being by interpretation King of righteousness, and after that also King of Salem, which is, King of peace."* You cannot out give God and you cannot out squeeze him either. You will go a lot further with the blessing of God on the ninety percent than you will with the curse of God on the one hundred percent. All of your tithes are to be given to the Pastor of this church. He is the one that God has appointed to be the under shepherd of your soul.

The blessings of a giver:
    Be faithful in giving and God will always give you more

than enough.

The greater your blessing, the more ways you should find to give: Freely ye have received, freely give.

God will bless you with more than money and possessions.

You can always depend upon His divine will.

There will be opposition but it will not stop you.

Others may mock you but God will exalt you.

God will honor and reward the giver.

Elisha was a living example of the principle that we are blessed to be a blessing. He did not think of his wants but looked at the hunger that the School of the Prophets at Gilgal was experiencing and told Gehazi to give them the bread to eat. 2 Corinthians 9:6-7 *"But this I say, He which soweth sparingly shall reap also sparingly; and he which soweth bountifully shall reap also bountifully. Every man according as he purposeth in his heart, so let him give; not grudgingly, or of necessity: for God loveth a cheerful giver."* Are you in love with the work of the Lord or just doing your duty?

Will He Ever Learn?

> 2 Kings 4:43-44 *"And his servitor said, What, should I set this before an hundred men? He said again, Give the people, that they may eat: for thus saith the LORD, They shall eat, and shall leave thereof. So he set it before them, and they did eat, and left thereof, according to the word of the LORD."*

Gehazi, Gehazi, will you ever learn? 2 Timothy 3:1-7 *"This know also, that in the last days perilous times shall come. For men shall be lovers of their own selves, covetous, boasters, proud, blasphemers, disobedient to parents, unthankful, unholy, Without natural affection, trucebreakers, false accusers, incontinent, fierce, despisers of those that are good, Traitors, heady, highminded, lovers of pleasures more than lovers of God; Having a form of godliness, but denying the power thereof: from such turn away. For of this sort are they which creep into houses, and lead captive silly women laden with sins, led away with divers lusts,* <u>*Ever learning, and never able to come to the knowledge of the truth.*</u>" Over and over he had seen God work miracles for the Prophet Elisha but he could not believe (a doubt driven by greed) that God would feed one hundred men with twenty barley loaves. So he opens his mouth and once again challenges the man of God. I cannot say it enough; God has given your Pastor so much wisdom that the best thing for you is to listen and obey what he teaches you. If you don't understand something, he is more than happy to explain it to you. But when you challenge his God given interpretation of the Word of God you are setting yourself up for failure.

The only miracle of Jesus that was recorded in all four gospel was the feeding of the 5,000 with the five loaves and two fishes. This miracle performed here by Elisha has the same elements as the one performed by Jesus.

The elements:

1. In each miracle there was a group of hungry people.

2. Elisha felt compassions for them, and Christ had compassion on the hungry multitude (Matthew 14:14).

3. A few loaves was the beginning of menu, and both times they were made from barley (John 6:9).

4. In each miracle they commanded their servant to give (not sell) to the people that they may eat (Mark 6:37).

5. In each case an unbelieving servant challenged them (John 6:7).

6. Elisha had his servant hand out the bread and Christ had the disciples hand out the bread (Matthew 14:19).

7. In each miracle they had leftovers after everyone had eaten (Matthew 14:20).

Our faith should never be paralyzed by the unbelief of others. We do not stand upon the wisdom of men but stand upon the promises of God. Jesus Christ is the same yesterday, today and forever. What he has done for other he will do for us too. Speak the language of faith and do no stumble. Because what God mandates He will always make a way for.

A Queen Who Saved The Day

Esther 4:13-14 *"Then Mordecai commanded to answer Esther, Think not with thyself that thou shalt escape in the king's house, more than all the Jews. For if thou altogether holdest thy peace at this time, then shall there enlargement and deliverance arise to the Jews from another place; but thou and thy father's house shall be destroyed: and who knoweth whether thou art come to the kingdom for such a time as this?"* It was the watershed moment of her life, the greatest opportunity of her service. The question was whether she would accept the challenge or would she run and hide. Thankfully she passed the test.   It was by her courageous faith that she became the deliverer of her people. We know that character is revealed by being tested but character is also revealed by advancement to power and position. Prosperity has done more to reveal character in our generation than adversity. Revelation 3:15-18 *"I know thy works, that thou art neither cold nor hot: I would thou wert cold or hot. So then because thou art lukewarm, and neither cold nor hot, I will spue thee out of my mouth. Because thou sayest, I am rich, and increased with goods, and have need of nothing; and knowest not that thou art wretched, and miserable, and poor, and blind, and naked: I counsel thee to buy of me gold tried in the fire, that thou mayest be rich; and white raiment, that thou mayest be clothed, and that the shame of thy nakedness do not appear; and anoint thine eyes with eyesalve, that thou mayest see."* When it is all said and done, what we do in a crisis hinges upon what we have been doing during the times of peace and prosperity.

Just like Esther was placed in the right place at the right time to save the day, the man from Baalshalisha was led by God to bring the bread that was needed for the next miracle. You too can be used by God to bring seeds of faith into people's life. God is looking for people just like me and you to do His work in the endtimes. It was not a complex or elaborate thing that the man from Baalshalisha did. It was just bringing some bread to the man of God. 2 Timothy 2:20-21 *"But in a great house there are not only vessels of gold and of silver, but also of wood and of earth; and some to honour, and some to dishonour. If a man therefore purge himself from these, he shall be a vessel unto honour, sanctified, and meet for the master's use, and prepared unto every good work."* If you will pray and seek God's face, He will use you too. You must have a desire to be a blessing and must love the truth with all your heart. Then get up out of your recliner and do something with eternal impact this week. Many times we defeat ourselves before we get started because we conclude that what we can do won't make a difference or reap any benefits. Everything you do for the Kingdom of God is a game changer for someone. At one point the only thing that Elisha did was pour water over the hands of Elijah when he washed them. But that was enough to get him an audience with the kings (2 Kings 3:11) when his time came.

Discussion Questions

1. What happen before Elisha feed the natural man?

2. Why was there poison in the pot?

3. Why did the man bring Elisha barley bread?

4. Who brought the barley bread to Elisha and Jesus?

5. What miracle is in all four gospels?

DOUBLE PORTION
The Miracles Of Elisha

Lesson Eight

The Walking Dead

This is the most famous miracle performed by the Prophet Elisha. While on earth, Jesus used the cleansing of the Leper Naaman as an example of those who had the Glory of God all around them but was not blessed by it because they considered it commonplace. Luke 4:22-30 *"And all bare him witness, and wondered at the gracious words which proceeded out of his mouth. And they said, Is not this Joseph's son? And he said unto them, Ye will surely say unto me this proverb, Physician, heal thyself: whatsoever we have heard done in Capernaum, do also here in thy country. And he said, Verily I say unto you, No prophet is accepted in his own country. But I tell you of a truth, many widows were in Israel in the days of Elias, when the heaven was shut up three years and six months, when great famine was throughout all the land; But unto none of them was Elias sent, save unto Sarepta, a city of Sidon, unto a woman that was a widow. And many lepers were in Israel in the time of Eliseus the prophet; and none of them was cleansed, saving Naaman the Syrian. And all they in the synagogue, when they heard these things, were filled with wrath, And rose up, and thrust him out of the city, and led him unto the brow of the hill whereon their city was built, that they might cast him down headlong. But he passing through the midst of them went his way."* (Note: The New Testament spelling of the name Elisha is Eliseus.) Under the Law of Moses, if a leper was healed of his leprosy, he had to go show himself to the priest before he was considered clean (Leviticus 14:2-32). There is not one example of a leper showing himself to the priest until Jesus healed the lepers (Luke 17:14). Other than Moses using leprosy as a demonstration of the power of God, I have found that only Elisha was used to heal a leper in the Old Testament. What we are studying today is a major event.

Scripture Text

2 Kings 5:1-20 *"Now Naaman, captain of the host of the king of Syria, was a great man with his master, and honourable, because by him the LORD had given deliverance unto Syria: he was also a mighty man in valour, but he was a leper. 2 And the Syrians had gone out by companies, and had brought away captive out of the land of Israel a little maid; and she waited on Naaman's wife. 3 And she said unto her mistress, Would God my lord were with the prophet that is in Samaria! for he would recover him of his leprosy. 4 And one went in, and told his lord, saying, Thus and thus said the maid that is of the land of Israel. 5 And the king of Syria said, Go to, go, and I will send a letter unto the king of Israel. And he departed, and took with him ten talents of silver, and six thousand pieces of gold, and ten changes of raiment. 6 And he brought the letter to the king of Israel, saying, Now when this letter is come unto thee, behold, I have therewith sent Naaman my servant to thee, that thou mayest recover him of his leprosy. 7 And it came to pass, when the king of Israel had read the letter, that he rent his clothes, and said, Am I God, to kill and to make alive, that this man doth send unto me to recover a man of his leprosy? wherefore consider, I pray you, and see how he seeketh a quarrel against me. 8 And it was so, when Elisha the man of God had heard that the king of Israel had rent his clothes, that he sent to the king, saying, Wherefore hast thou rent thy clothes? let him come now to me, and he shall know that there is a prophet in Israel. 9 So Naaman came with his horses and with his chariot, and stood at the door of the house of Elisha. 10 And Elisha sent a messenger unto him, saying, Go and wash in Jordan seven times, and thy flesh shall come again to thee, and thou shalt be clean. 11 But Naaman was wroth, and went away, and said, Behold, I thought, He will surely come out to me, and stand, and call on the name of the LORD his God, and strike his hand over the place, and recover the leper. 12 Are not Abana and Pharpar, rivers of Damascus, better than all the waters of Israel? may I not*

wash in them, and be clean? So he turned and went away in a rage. 13 And his servants came near, and spake unto him, and said, My father, if the prophet had bid thee do some great thing, wouldest thou not have done it? how much rather then, when he saith to thee, Wash, and be clean? 14 Then went he down, and dipped himself seven times in Jordan, according to the saying of the man of God: and his flesh came again like unto the flesh of a little child, and he was clean. 15 And he returned to the man of God, he and all his company, and came, and stood before him: and he said, Behold, now I know that there is no God in all the earth, but in Israel: now therefore, I pray thee, take a blessing of thy servant. 16 But he said, As the LORD liveth, before whom I stand, I will receive none. And he urged him to take it; but he refused. 17 And Naaman said, Shall there not then, I pray thee, be given to thy servant two mules' burden of earth? for thy servant will henceforth offer neither burnt offering nor sacrifice unto other gods, but unto the LORD. 18 In this thing the LORD pardon thy servant, that when my master goeth into the house of Rimmon to worship there, and he leaneth on my hand, and I bow myself in the house of Rimmon: when I bow down myself in the house of Rimmon, the LORD pardon thy servant in this thing. 19 And he said unto him, Go in peace. So he departed from him a little way. 20 But Gehazi, the servant of Elisha the man of God, said, Behold, my master hath spared Naaman this Syrian, in not receiving at his hands that which he brought: but, as the LORD liveth, I will run after him, and take somewhat of him"

Naaman The Leper

> 2 Kings 5:1 *"Now Naaman, captain of the host of the king of Syria, was a great man with his master, and honourable, because by him the LORD had given deliverance unto Syria: he was also a mighty man in valour, but he was a leper."*

Naaman was a great man because the Lord had given him victory in battle. He was also highly regarded by the king of Syria for his bravery. We can learn from this today that God can orchestrate success in all walks of life. Even though Naaman worshiped the idol Rimmon, God saw the heart of Naaman and worked events to lead him to God. In no way should we think that temporal success is a stamp of God's approval. God at times will use the wicked to fulfill His plan. He will also use success to test the heart of man.

But none of this success made up for the fact that Naaman had a painful death sentence upon his head, he was a leper. Remember, the enemy and mankind always identifies you by your sin or illness (Naaman the Leper), but God identifies you as a child of God (Luke 8:48).

Leprosy

The best parallel to leprosy in the Bible is sin in the world today. By examining leprosy we will come to a better understating of the battle we are facing today. One fact that we know about sin is that is separates man from God. So if we can have a better understanding of sin, we have a better arsenals of spiritual weapons to defeat sin.

1. Leprosy in the beginning appears to be no big deal. The symptoms are so insignificant that a person can easily hide them from everyone else. The symptoms are a little different from person to person. Leviticus 13:2 *"When a man shall have in the skin of his flesh a rising, a scab, or bright spot, and it be in the skin of his flesh like the plague of leprosy; then he shall be brought unto Aaron the priest, or unto one of his sons the priests."*

    To the world today sin is no big deal. You will hear it time and time again, God is not going to send me to Hell over that. They even go so far as to tell you to forget about your sins of yesterday so you won't feel guilty about committing them today. Just like Adam and Eve hid from God in the garden, most people today start out by hiding their sins from everyone else. Not every person has the same temptations. But most of the time people are tripped up by power, sex or money. 1 John 2:16 *"For all that is in the world, the lust of the flesh, and the lust of the eyes, and the pride of life, is not of the Father, but is of the world."*

2. Leprosy is a very contagious disease that can be inherited. It can be passed through the blood from mother to baby.

    How tragic it is to see the parents teaching their children to sin. What would cause a mother to tell her children to steal candy at the store because they won't do nothing to a child if they get caught? We have a world today where the parents are dragging their children into the same filth they are mired down in. They have turned the minds of their children over to demented, possessed and perverted. Who is it that is teaching and entertaining your children?

3. The noticeable effects of leprosy progress very slowly. At the beginning there is only slight pain. It is only after it has taken over that the repulsive mutation of the body begins.

    The spiral into the pits of Hell is a very gradual process. First man is exposed to sin, then he becomes curious about the sin, next he partakes of the sin, then it becomes addicted to the sin, which causes him to sear his conscience and at last he justifies his sin by proclaiming that he was born that way. 1 Timothy 4:1-2 *"Now the Spirit speaketh expressly, that in the latter times some shall depart from the faith, giving heed to seducing spirits, and doctrines of devils; Speaking lies in hypocrisy; having their conscience seared with a hot iron."* At first man partakes of sin and it appears that nothing bad has happen. For some they feel a rush from doing something wrong and getting away with it. But did they really get away with it? Ecclesiastes 8:11 *"Because sentence against an evil work is not executed speedily, therefore the heart of the sons of men is fully set in them to do evil."*

4. Leprosy creates the real walking dead. The color of the skin is altered, the body is covered with open sores and the worst of all is the loss of feeling in the hands, feet and other parts of the body. A leper can burn his hand off in the fire and never feel the pain that would cause a normal person to pull back. It can also destroy the vision making the person go blind.

    Sin deceives man into thinking that he is really living while in fact he is being wrapped in the bondage of living death. 1 Timothy 5:6 *"But she that liveth in pleasure is dead while she liveth."* How scary it must be to know that there is a God and you cannot feel Him. Our world today no longer feels bad about their open and uncontrolled sin. Ephesians 2:1-3 *"And you hath he quickened, who were dead in trespasses and sins; Wherein in time past ye walked according to the course of this world, according to the prince of the power of the air, the spirit that now worketh in the children of disobedience: Among whom also we all had our conversation in times past in the lusts of our flesh, fulfilling the desires of the flesh and of the mind; and were by nature the children of wrath, even as others."*

5. Once leprosy takes root, it spreads very rapidly throughout the body. Not only does it spread on the exterior of the body, it also moves internal to affect the bone structure of the body.

 Sin will eventually spread to every aspect of a man's life. In the end every part of a man's soul will be corrupted. There is nothing that man will not do to be able to continue his sin. Sin will always take you further than you ever intended to go and keep you longer than you ever intended to stay and cost you more than you can ever afford to pay. 2 Peter 2:18-19 *"For when they speak great swelling words of vanity, they allure through the lusts of the flesh, through much wantonness, those that were clean escaped from them who live in error. While they promise them liberty, they themselves are the servants of corruption: for of whom a man is overcome, of the same is he brought in bondage."*

6. When one was diagnosed with leprosy they were placed outside the camp. Leviticus 13:46 *"All the days wherein the plague shall be in him he shall be defiled; he is unclean: he shall dwell alone; without the camp shall his habitation be."*

Sin must not be pampered and expected inside the church today. We must teach and preach against sin. Sin will remove you from the Glory of God. 2 Thessalonians 1:8-9 *"In flaming fire taking vengeance on them that know not God, and that obey not the gospel of our Lord Jesus Christ: Who shall be punished with everlasting destruction from the presence of the Lord, and from the glory of his power."* At the end of the day, sin will leave you lonely, surrounded by evil and deceived into thinking that the church doesn't want you back.

A Hope That Sprang Eternal

2 Kings 5:2-4 "And the Syrians had gone out by companies,

and had brought away captive out of the land of Israel a little maid; and she waited on Naaman's wife. 3 And she said unto her mistress, Would God my lord were with the prophet that is in Samaria! for he would recover him of his leprosy. 4 And one went in, and told his lord, saying, Thus and thus said the maid that is of the land of Israel."

There was a little maid who had every right to hate Naaman. He had taken her captive and dragged her miles from home to be his slave. But somewhere within her, the love of God was greater than her circumstance and she demonstrated the principle of doing good to those who despitefully use you. Matthew 5:44-46 *"But I say unto you, Love your enemies, bless them that curse you, do good to them that hate you, and pray for them which despitefully use you, and persecute you; That ye may be the children of your Father which is in heaven: for he maketh his sun to rise on the evil and on the good, and sendeth rain on the just and on the unjust. For if ye love them which love you, what reward have ye? do not even the publicans the same?"*

It is interesting to note that the maid said nothing about going to see the king of Syria or the king of Israel. She told him that it was a prophet and he lived in Samaria. We will save ourselves a lot of heartache if we listen and do what the Pastor preaches.

In today's economy the gift that Naaman was willing to give to Elisha was worth well over a million dollars. I believe Naaman intentions were innocent and he believed he would have to pay for his healing. But many today are using money to influence the quote, unquote man of God. Acts 8:18-21 *"And when Simon saw that through laying on of the apostles' hands the Holy Ghost was given, he offered them money, Saying, Give me also this power, that on whomsoever I lay hands, he may receive the Holy Ghost. But Peter said unto him, Thy money perish with thee, because thou hast thought that the gift of God may be purchased with money. Thou hast neither part nor lot in this matter: for thy heart is not right in the sight of God."*

How Stupid Can You Get?

2 Kings 5:6 *"And he brought the letter to the king of Israel, saying, Now when this letter is come unto thee, behold, I have therewith sent Naaman my servant to thee, that thou*

mayest recover him of his leprosy. 7 And it came to pass, when the king of Israel had read the letter, that he rent his clothes, and said, Am I God, to kill and to make alive, that this man doth send unto me to recover a man of his leprosy? wherefore consider, I pray you, and see how he seeketh a quarrel against me. 8 And it was so, when Elisha the man of God had heard that the king of Israel had rent his clothes, that he sent to the king, saying, Wherefore hast thou rent thy clothes? let him come now to me, and he shall know that there is a prophet in Israel."

The king of Israel had already forgotten the great miracle that the prophet Elisha had performed for him in the desert. Because of his evil heart he had no confidence in the one true God. If he had been like King Hezekiah (2 Kings 19:14) and taken the letter into the temple and put it on the altar and prayed for God's wisdom he would have known what to do. This passage illustrate how at this time man considered leprosy an incurable disease. The Lord did freely speak to Elisha and reveal things unto him (like he speaks to the Pastor of the church), so rather than being insulted by the stupid king, he had mercy on the hurting and ask the king to send Naaman to him. Even if the king of Israel was too stupid to remember that there was a prophet in Israel, God was going to show it once again unto Syria.

The Miracle

2 Kings 9:14 *"So Naaman came with his horses and with his chariot, and stood at the door of the house of Elisha. 10 And Elisha sent a messenger unto him, saying, Go and wash in Jordan seven times, and thy flesh shall come again to thee, and thou shalt be clean. 11 But Naaman was wroth, and went away, and said, Behold, I thought, He will surely come out to me, and stand, and call on the name of the LORD his God, and strike his hand over the place, and recover the leper. 12 Are not Abana and Pharpar, rivers of Damascus, better than all the waters of Israel? may I not wash in them, and be clean? So he turned and went away in a rage. 13 And his servants came near, and spake unto him, and said, My father, if the prophet had bid thee do some great thing, wouldest thou not have done it? how much rather then, when he saith to thee, Wash, and be clean? 14 Then went he down, and dipped himself*

> *seven times in Jordan, according to the saying of the man of God: and his flesh came again like unto the flesh of a little child, and he was clean."*

There was no problem too small or any task too great for the Prophet Elisha. He loved people but had no desire to feed the pride of the self-important. Also he wanted to demonstrate that it was not the vessel that God used (the messenger) but it was God and the message that was important. 1 Corinthians 3:5-6 *"Who then is Paul, and who is Apollos, but ministers by whom ye believed, even as the Lord gave to every man? I have planted, Apollos watered; but God gave the increase."* It is not healthy for the global church to have super preachers to whom people give more credence than their Pastor. The man God uses to speak into your life is your Pastor and no one has a greater word from the Lord than him.

The call to be cleansed from sin is still a revolting thought to the carnal man. Naaman's ego was bruised and his proud spirit rose up in him to revolt against the command of God. His carnality spoke to demonstrate the audacity of man to tell God what is best. Like a dog chasing his tail, the children of Israel was constantly forsaking the Word of God to do what was right in their own eyes. This proud and rebellious spirit always brought them back into bondage. Naaman's outburst is like the guilty trying to dictate to the judge how he should be treated. So many in our world today are constantly getting into trouble with God because they live life believing they deserve happiness, power and wealth. Just hope you don't get what you deserve but that God has mercy on you. Romans 6:23 *"For the wages of sin is death…"* You will find a lot more peace and contentment in life when you begin to count your blessing rather than demand your rights.

The Jordan River should never have been an issue to Naaman. It was the river that God and Elisha had used before to demonstrate the power of God. The Jordan River became the test of obedience for Naaman because of his pride. You will be tested in your walk with God. God wants to know if you will obey him even when you don't understand why you are asked to do it. We will never be accepted by God unless we humble ourselves at an old fashion altar and call out to God on a regular basis. 1 Peter 5:5 *"…For God resisteth the proud, and giveth grace to the humble."*

May we all be so blessed to have a friend that will help us see the obvious when we are overrun with emotions. Many times the enemy will blow the requirements for miraculous living way out of proportion. Compared to the glory we will obtain, what the Lord ask of us is always a small thing. You will never have God fail you or forsake you. Naaman dipped himself seven times. The number seven in the Bible is referred to as the number of completion. It was on the seventh day that creation was complete and God entered into fellowship with man. When Naaman obeyed the commandment of Elisha, his cleansing was instantaneous and complete. This was not just a partial healing but God completely healed Naaman of his leprosy. All power in heaven and in earth is in the name of Jesus. When we call upon the name of Jesus, we can expect complete healing, complete deliverance and complete victory. This miracle was wroth by a tremendous act of trust and faith on the part of Naaman. No one, notta, zip, zero in the land of Israel was healed of leprosy by Elisha because they refused to believe the man of God. To hear the voice of the Lord through the vessel he has chosen is required to partake of the miraculous. That is the voice of your Pastor. God only uses an anointed vessel to do His work. Quit listening to the parking lot prophets and Jezebels, they are the ones who got Israel into this mess in the first place.

Holy Ground

> 2 Kings 5:15-19 *"And he returned to the man of God, he and all his company, and came, and stood before him: and he said, Behold, now I know that there is no God in all the earth, but in Israel: now therefore, I pray thee, take a blessing of thy servant. 16 But he said, As the LORD liveth, before whom I stand, I will receive none. And he urged him to take it; but he refused. 17 And Naaman said, Shall there not then, I pray thee, be given to thy servant two mules' burden of earth? for thy servant will henceforth offer neither burnt offering nor sacrifice unto other gods, but unto the LORD. 18 In this thing the LORD pardon thy servant, that when my master goeth into the house of Rimmon to worship there, and he leaneth on my hand, and I bow myself in the house of Rimmon: when I bow down myself in the house of Rimmon, the LORD pardon thy servant in this thing. 19 And he said unto him, Go in peace. So he departed from him a little way."*

Naaman returned to Elisha a changed man. Once you experience the miraculous you will never want to go back to the ordinary of yesterday. Not only will believers speak in other tongues as the Spirit gives utterance when they receive the Holy Ghost, they will also have a glow of the peace and joy of the Lord. When the Glory of God descends and fills your temple (1 Kings 8:11) no one can deny the demonstration of transformation. Romans 12:1-2 "*I beseech you therefore, brethren, by the mercies of God, that ye present your bodies a living sacrifice, holy, acceptable unto God, which is your reasonable service. And be not conformed to this world: but be ye transformed by the renewing of your mind, that ye may prove what is that good, and acceptable, and perfect, will of God.*"

Elisha refused to accept the million dollars' worth of gifts from Namaan. This was to prove to Syria that the one true God did not take gifts like Rimmon in order to bless His People. To this day men bring precious gifts to idols, thinking it will cause the idols to bless them, just like the Syrians did to their idol Rimmon. God is the one who blesses us, he does not take blessings from us in order give us favor. We worship and praise God because we love him. The blessing that we receive when we offer up a sacrifice of praise cannot be bought with money or gifts. Hebrews 13:15 "*By him therefore let us offer the sacrifice of praise to God continually, that is, the fruit of our lips giving thanks to his name.*" We no longer offer a sacrifice of goats and bullocks but now we offer a sacrifice of praise. If you want God to bless you, then it is time to get your praise on.

At first glance it seems an odd request that Namaan made. He ask for two mules loaded down with dirt from Elisha lawn. But in reality it shows a revelation that Namaan had about God using only holy things. He wanted to take home some of the holy ground to worship God upon. What a switch Namman had made, from preferring the Abana and Pharpar, rivers of Damascus to wanting the dirt of Israel. When we come to God the things we once loved we will now hate and the things we once hated we will now love. Holiness is the revealed nature of God and His love draws us to become more like Him. If we are ever going to see Jesus in heaven, we must live a holy life here on earth. Hebrews 12:14 "*Follow peace with all men, and holiness, without which no man shall see the Lord.*"

The last part of the passage needs to be looked at as a confession of what Naaman had done in the past and now he realized it was wrong. He was asking God for forgiveness of the times he went with the king to bow down to Rimmon. Elisha's parting gift was peace. Philippians 4:6-9 *"Be careful for nothing; but in every thing by prayer and supplication with thanksgiving let your requests be made known unto God. And the peace of God, which passeth all understanding, shall keep your hearts and minds through Christ Jesus. Finally, brethren, whatsoever things are true, whatsoever things are honest, whatsoever things are just, whatsoever things are pure, whatsoever things are lovely, whatsoever things are of good report; if there be any virtue, and if there be any praise, think on these things. Those things, which ye have both learned, and received, and heard, and seen in me, do: and the God of peace shall be with you."*

Discussion Questions

1. What did Jesus have to say about this miracle?

____

____

____

2. Why is leprosy like sin?

____

____

____

3. Why did Naaman take dirt home with him?

____

____

____

4. Who told Naaman about the prophet in Samaria?

____

____

____

5. What begins to happen when man spirals into the pits of Hell?

____

____

____

Double Portion
The Miracles Of Elisha

Lesson Nine

Forsaken Glory

I remember when my father entered into the Bishop stage of his ministry, he never missed the opportunity to impart a word of wisdom into your life. 1 Corinthians 12:7-11 *"But the manifestation of the Spirit is given to every man to profit withal. For to one is given by the Spirit the word of wisdom; to another the word of knowledge by the same Spirit; To another faith by the same Spirit; to another the gifts of healing by the same Spirit; To another the working of miracles; to another prophecy; to another discerning of spirits; to another divers kinds of tongues; to another the interpretation of tongues: But all these worketh that one and the selfsame Spirit, dividing to every man severally as he will."* I may have been stopping by to pick up some home grown tomatoes, but he saw it as an opportunity to quote a scripture that was relevant for the moment or remind me of a principal from the Word of God. It did not matter who you was, when you came into his world he was going to allow the works of the Spirit to flow. He spend more time preaching to the doctors than they spent practicing medicine on him. He also had a side project where he took a man under his wing who had no knowledge of God and made it his mission to pour God into him on a daily basis. Ministry starts one on one and it is designed to always have one on one. Psalms 23:1-6 *"The LORD is my shepherd; I shall not want. He maketh me to lie down in green pastures: he leadeth me beside the still waters. He restoreth my soul: he leadeth me in the paths of righteousness for his name's sake. Yea, though I walk through the valley of the shadow of death, I will fear no evil: for thou art with me; thy rod and thy staff they comfort me. Thou preparest a table before me in the presence of mine enemies: thou anointest my head with oil; my cup runneth over. Surely goodness and mercy shall follow me all the days of my life: and I will dwell in the house of the LORD for ever."* The Glory of God can follow you all the days of your life.

Just like Eve was deceived into forsaking the glory of paradise, the enemy of your soul wants to trick you into forsaking the Glory of God. When we are born of the water and of the Spirit we are given a glimpse into the eternal glory. The beauty and atmosphere of heaven will leave you awe struck every time you read about it. Revelation 21:11-21 *"Having the glory of God: and her light was like unto a stone most precious, even like a jasper stone, clear as crystal; And had a wall great and high, and had twelve gates, and at the gates twelve angels, and names written thereon, which are the names of the twelve tribes of the children of Israel: On the east three gates; on the north three gates; on the south three gates; and on the west three gates. And the wall of the city had twelve foundations, and in them the names of the twelve apostles of the Lamb. And he that talked with me had a golden reed to measure the city, and the gates thereof, and the wall thereof. And the city lieth foursquare, and the length is as large as the breadth: and he measured the city with the reed, twelve thousand furlongs. The length and the breadth and the height of it are equal. And he measured the wall thereof, an hundred and forty and four cubits, according to the measure of a man, that is, of the angel. And the building of the wall of it was of jasper: and the city was pure gold, like unto clear glass. And the foundations of the wall of the city were garnished with all manner of precious stones. The first foundation was jasper; the second, sapphire; the third, a chalcedony; the fourth, an emerald; The fifth, sardonyx; the sixth, sardius; the seventh, chrysolite; the eighth, beryl; the ninth, a topaz; the tenth, a chrysoprasus; the eleventh, a jacinth; the twelfth, an amethyst. And the twelve gates were twelve pearls; every several gate was of one pearl: and the street of the city was pure gold, as it were transparent glass."* Why would anyone want to take a chance on missing all of this?

How many miss out on the blessings of God because they are lured by the temptation of wealth and possessions. They take jobs to make more money and miss church services. They work long hours and neglect the spiritual upkeep of their families. When is it that financial gain is worth more that spiritual advancement? Luke 16:13 *"No servant can serve two masters: for either he will hate the one, and love the other; or else he will hold to the one, and despise the other. Ye cannot serve God and mammon."* In the end they wind up regretting it because they realize they have forsaken the Glory of God for mammon. Every one of us will be tested to see if we love God more than money. The only way to pass this test is to set our priorities according to the Word of God. Matthew 6:31-33 *"Therefore take no thought, saying, What shall we eat? or, What shall we drink? or, Wherewithal shall we be clothed? (For after all these things do the Gentiles seek:) for your heavenly Father knoweth that ye have need of all these things. But seek ye first the kingdom of God, and his righteousness; and all these things shall be added unto you."* We are not saying that God will not bring financial blessings into your life. We have several examples of God blessing people so they can further the work of the Lord. We are saying to put God first and the call will bring the blessings.

It is just heart wrenching to see what man has traded the Glory of God for. To some it was a pack of cigarettes, a ten minute fling in a motel room, a few more dollars in the paycheck, a new fishing boat, the thrill of the gaming tables, the vibrating beat of the music or the entertainments of Hell, etc. Matthew 16:26 *"For what is a man profited, if he shall gain the whole world, and lose his own soul? or what shall a man give in exchange for his soul?"* Don't ever put a price on your soul because if you do, the day will come when the enemy will steal your soul. The enemy will never keep his end of the bargain but he still ends up with your soul and you die lost.

Scripture Text

2 Kings 5:21-27 *"So Gehazi followed after Naaman. And when Naaman saw him running after him, he lighted down from the chariot to meet him, and said, Is all well? 22 And he said, All is well. My master hath sent me, saying, Behold, even now there be*

come to me from mount Ephraim two young men of the sons of the prophets: give them, I pray thee, a talent of silver, and two changes of garments. 23 And Naaman said, Be content, take two talents. And he urged him, and bound two talents of silver in two bags, with two changes of garments, and laid them upon two of his servants; and they bare them before him. 24 And when he came to the tower, he took them from their hand, and bestowed them in the house: and he let the men go, and they departed. 25 But he went in, and stood before his master. And Elisha said unto him, Whence comest thou, Gehazi? And he said, Thy servant went no whither. 26 And he said unto him, Went not mine heart with thee, when the man turned again from his chariot to meet thee? Is it a time to receive money, and to receive garments, and oliveyards, and vineyards, and sheep, and oxen, and menservants, and maidservants? 27 The leprosy therefore of Naaman shall cleave unto thee, and unto thy seed for ever. And he went out from his presence a leper as white as snow."

Who Was Gehazi?

Gehazi was the main servant of Elisha at this time. Gehazi was the apparent successor of the Prophet Elisha, just like Elisha was the successor to Elijah. The dictionary translates the name Gehazi as "valley of vision." This name is almost a contradiction. In order to see what was going on, a lookout would typically perch on a mountain and not sit in a valley. Spiritual visions also befell people mostly on mountains, and valleys were typically known as areas where things could be hidden and not seen. 2 Corinthians 4:1-6 *"Therefore seeing we have this ministry, as we have received mercy, we faint not; But have renounced the hidden things of dishonesty, not walking in craftiness, nor handling the word of God deceitfully; but by manifestation of the truth commending ourselves to every man's conscience in the sight of God. But if our gospel be hid, it is hid to them that are lost: In whom the god of this world hath blinded the minds of them which believe not, lest the light of the glorious gospel of Christ, who is the image of God, should shine unto them. For we preach not ourselves, but Christ Jesus the Lord; and ourselves your servants for Jesus' sake. For God, who commanded the light to shine out of darkness, hath shined in our hearts, to give the light of the knowledge of the glory of God in the face of Jesus Christ."* The name Gehazi seems to illustrate a person being in the wrong place for the wrong reasons. Living in the valley of doubt can cause you to follow the wrong visions.

Gehazi had left a long trail of doubt, greed, contempt, and rebellion in his wake. He had tried to manhandle the Shunammite woman, was not able to use the staff of Elisha to raise the Shunammite woman's son from death because of his unbelief. Some of his greed showed through when he expressed dissention about Elisha using the barley bread to feed the one hundred sons of the prophets. Now that Elisha had refused over a million dollars' worth of gifts, Gehazi greed overtook him just like it did in Judas. The Bible tells us that both of them were thieves. John 12:1-8 *"Then Jesus six days before the passover came to Bethany, where Lazarus was which had been dead, whom he raised from the dead. There they made him a supper; and Martha served: but Lazarus was one of them that sat at the table with him. Then took Mary a pound of ointment of spikenard, very costly, and anointed the feet of Jesus, and wiped his feet with her hair: and the house was filled with the odour of the ointment. Then saith one of his disciples, Judas Iscariot, Simon's son, which should betray him, Why was not this ointment sold for three hundred pence, and given to the poor? This he said, not that he cared for the poor; but because he was a thief, and had the bag, and bare what was put therein. Then said Jesus, Let her alone: against the day of my burying hath she kept this. For the poor always ye have with you; but me ye have not always."* Suddenly he allowed the enemy to discount all the honor, grace and Glory of God to nothing in order to fulfill his lust. He was without excuse, he knew about and had experienced the miraculous power of God. Romans 1:18-21 *"For the wrath of God is revealed from heaven against all ungodliness and unrighteousness of men, who hold the truth in unrighteousness; Because that which may be known of God is manifest in them; for God hath shewed it unto them. For the invisible things of him from the creation of the world are clearly seen, being understood by the things that are made, even his eternal power and Godhead; so that they are without excuse: Because that, when they knew God, they glorified him not as God, neither were thankful; but became vain in their imaginations, and their foolish heart was darkened."*

On The Road To Destruction

2 Kings 5:21-23 *"So Gehazi followed after Naaman. And when Naaman saw him running after him, he lighted down from the chariot to meet him, and said, Is all well? 22 And he said, All is well. My master hath sent me, saying, Behold, even now there be come to me from mount Ephraim two young men of the sons of the prophets: give them, I pray thee, a talent of silver, and two changes of garments. 23 And Naaman said, Be content, take two talents. And he urged him, and bound two talents of silver in two bags, with two changes of garments, and laid them upon two of his servants; and they bare them before him."*

Gehazi's greedy heart caused him to run after Naaman. He now resorts to lies in order to convince Naaman that Elisha sent him to get goods for the sons of the prophets. All lies have some truth in them. So Gehazi uses the established Schools of the Prophets as a pretense for his lies. Naaman was a changed man and gave Gehazi more than he ask for. Gehazi was probably congratulating himself on how well his scheme had worked, thinking he was now on easy street. But il-gotten gain will cause pain and suffering as long as you hold on to it. Proverbs 21:6 *"The getting of treasures by a lying tongue is a vanity tossed to and fro of them that seek death."*

Gehazi was the student of the Prophet Elisha, and Judas Iscariot was the student of Jesus Christ. Both of them walked and talked with their teacher every day. What was it that caused them to forsake the Glory of God for such temporary gain? Somewhere along the path they begin to listen to seducing spirits. Mark 13:22 *"For false Christs and false prophets shall rise, and shall shew signs and wonders, to seduce, if it were possible, even the elect."* A seducing spirit is one that will not take no for an answer but will just keep coming back until it is cast out. This spirit gets its foothold when greed drives us to covet the blessing of others. How did Gehazi and Judas, who were blessed beyond our comprehension succumb to such temptation? Luke 21:34-36 *"And take heed to yourselves, lest at any time your hearts be overcharged with surfeiting, and drunkenness, and cares of this life, and so that day come upon you unawares. For as a snare shall it come on all them that dwell on the face of the whole earth. Watch ye therefore, and pray always, that ye may be accounted worthy to escape all these things that shall come to pass, and to stand before the Son of man."* Paul had a young minister that he had great confidence in. Paul was grooming Demas to be a great minister of the gospel. How could anyone walk away from the great tutelage of the Apostle Paul? 2 Timothy 4:10 *"For Demas hath forsaken me, having loved this present world, and is departed unto Thessalonica..."* To forsake the glory of God for a temporary worldly thrill will bring regret and despair for the rest of your life. Did they not realize that they were being groomed for a powerful ministry of eternal impact? All of them had great talents and unlimited potential. If they would have just been faithful for a while longer they could have become men of renown.

In contrast we have those who have made the decision to forsake the world and found the great riches of the Kingdom of God. Hebrews 11:23-29 *"By faith Moses, when he was born, was hid three months of his parents, because they saw he was a proper child; and they were not afraid of the king's commandment. By faith Moses, when he was come to years, refused to be called the son of Pharaoh's daughter; Choosing rather to suffer affliction with the people of God, than to enjoy the pleasures of sin for a season; Esteeming the reproach of Christ greater riches than the treasures in Egypt: for he had respect unto the recompence of the reward. By faith he forsook Egypt, not fearing the wrath of the king: for he endured, as seeing him who is invisible. Through faith he kept the passover, and the sprinkling of blood, lest he that destroyed the firstborn should touch them. By faith they passed through the Red sea as by dry land: which the Egyptians assaying to do were drowned."* Moses was able to forsake Egypt because he was able to see the invisible riches of the reward to come. The pleasures of sin are always temporary and will bring a bitter reward of regret. As long as we keep our eyes on Jesus we will never be tempted to forsake the glory of God. It is when we get our eyes on man that we will begin to stumble.

We have those who throughout history have faltered and lost all just before the finish line. There was a man in the early day of our country who had a great lineage and a great education. At first glance, one would expect him to be among the foremost of America's famous founding fathers. He was the grandson of the well-known theologian Jonathan Edwards and the son of the president of Princeton University. He served as a soldier in the Revolutionary War and was an officer on the staff of George Washington for some time. Later he was elected as a United States senator from the state of New York, and his political career was on the rise. He almost succeeded as a national Presidential candidate in the election of 1800, coming within one electoral vote of being elected President in this hotly disputed contest. He finally settled for the vice-presidency under Thomas Jefferson.

Had his life ended before 1804, the name of Aaron Burr would have been spoken with admiration and honor instead of scorn and contempt. But after mortally wounding Alexander Hamilton in a pistol duel and then conspiring with the British government to set up an independent government west of the Mississippi River, he came to be considered in the same manner as the likes of Benedict Arnold. Words like crook, traitor and worse were applied to him. Instead of being remembered as an honored leader of the United States, he was remembered for his acts of betrayal.

Hiding From God

> 2 Kings 5:24-26 *"And when he came to the tower, he took them from their hand, and bestowed them in the house: and he let the men go, and they departed. 25 But he went in, and stood before his master. And Elisha said unto him, Whence comest thou, Gehazi? And he said, Thy servant went no whither. 26 And he said unto him, Went not mine heart with thee, when the man turned again from his chariot to meet thee? Is it a time to receive money, and to receive garments, and oliveyards, and vineyards, and sheep, and oxen, and menservants, and maidservants?*

Gehazi cared little that he had brought a reproach upon the name of God and Elisha but was determined to thumb his nose at God and consume his ill-gotten gain. 1 Timothy 3:1-7 *"This is a true saying, If a man desire the office of a bishop, he desireth a good* work.   A bishop then must be blameless, the husband of one wife, vigilant, sober, of good behaviour, given to hospitality, apt to teach; Not given to wine, no striker, not greedy of filthy lucre; but patient, not a brawler, not covetous; One that ruleth well his own house, having his children in subjection with all gravity; (For if a man know not how to rule his own house, how shall he take care of the church of God?) Not a novice, lest being lifted up with pride he fall into the condemnation of the devil. Moreover he must have a good report of them which are without; lest he fall into reproach and the snare of the devil." Gehazi could not blame his failure on bad leadership. He had the best group of people in the land to work with, The Schools of the Prophets. He just allowed an evil spirit to enter into his life. His transgressions didn't make senses but sin never makes sense. He then compounded his misery by trying to hide his theft from Elisha. This approach did not work well for Achan either.   Joshua 7:19-26 *"And Joshua said unto Achan, My son, give, I pray thee, glory to the LORD God of Israel, and make confession unto him; and tell me now what thou hast done; hide it not from me. And Achan answered Joshua, and said, Indeed I have sinned against the LORD God of Israel, and thus and thus have I done: When I saw among the spoils a goodly Babylonish garment, and two hundred shekels of silver, and a wedge of gold of fifty shekels weight, then I coveted them, and took them; and, behold, they are hid in the earth in the midst of my tent, and the silver under it. So Joshua sent messengers, and they ran unto the tent; and, behold, it was hid in his tent, and the silver under it. And they took them out of the midst of the tent, and brought them unto Joshua, and unto all the children of Israel, and laid them out before the LORD. And Joshua, and all Israel with him, took Achan the son of Zerah, and the silver, and the garment, and the wedge of gold, and his sons, and his daughters, and his oxen, and his asses, and his sheep, and his tent, and all that he had: and they brought them unto the valley of Achor. And Joshua said, Why hast thou troubled us? the LORD shall trouble thee this day. And all Israel stoned him with stones, and burned them with fire, after they had stoned them with stones. And they raised over him a great heap of stones unto this day. So the LORD turned from the fierceness of his anger. Wherefore the name of that place was called, The valley of Achor, unto this day."*

It appears from the words of Elisha that God had revealed unto him that Gehazi intended to take his ill-gotten gain and leave

Elisha and set himself up as a farmer. Elisha mentioned that Gehazi had missed God's timing. Let us patiently wait for God to unfold His will for our life and we will get the desires of our heart. Psalms 37:3-7 *"Trust in the LORD, and do good; so shalt thou dwell in the land, and verily thou shalt be fed. Delight thyself also in the LORD; and he shall give thee the desires of thine heart. Commit thy way unto the LORD; trust also in him; and he shall bring it to pass. And he shall bring forth thy righteousness as the light, and thy judgment as the noonday. Rest in the LORD, and wait patiently for him: fret not thyself because of him who prospereth in his way, because of the man who bringeth wicked devices to pass."* That beautiful farm could have been Gehazi someday. When we forsake the Glory, we also forsake our dreams.

The Glory Of God Has Departed

2 Kings 5:27 *"The leprosy therefore of Naaman shall cleave unto thee, and unto thy seed for ever. And he went out from his presence a leper as white as snow."*

What a sorrowful ending to a man whose destiny was to become the next prophet of Israel. He coveted the things of Naaman and he got what Naaman wanted rid of more than anything else, his leprosy. He handed his sin on to his children and they suffered the same punishment of leprosy. The way you break the curse of sin is to repent of your sins and you will become a new man. To some this judgement may seem harsh. But we need to remember Ananias and Sapphira who lied to the man of God, which was receiving a gift for the Kingdom of God from them. Acts 5:1-11 *"But a certain man named Ananias, with Sapphira his wife, sold a possession, And kept back part of the price, his wife also being privy to it, and brought a certain part, and laid it at the apostles' feet. But Peter said, Ananias, why hath Satan filled thine heart to lie to the Holy Ghost, and to keep back part of the price of the land? Whiles it remained, was it not thine own? and after it was sold, was it not in thine own power? why hast thou conceived this thing in thine heart? thou hast not lied unto men, but unto God. And Ananias hearing these words fell down, and gave up the ghost: and great fear came on all them that heard these things. And the young men arose, wound him up, and carried him out, and buried him. And it was about the space of three hours after, when his wife, not knowing what was done, came in. And Peter answered unto her, Tell me whether ye sold the land for so much? And she said, Yea, for so much. Then Peter said unto her, How is it that ye have agreed together to tempt the Spirit of the Lord? behold, the feet of them which have buried thy husband are at the door, and shall carry thee out. Then fell she down straightway at his feet, and yielded up the ghost: and the young men came in, and found her dead, and, carrying her forth, buried her by her husband. And great fear came upon all the church, and upon as many as heard these things."* These are stark reminders that every one of us are going to stand before God and be judged and there are times on earth when the balance is tripped and judgement is pour out right then.

Discussion Questions

1. What is the first think mentioned in Revelation 21:11?

____

____

____

2. Why did Gehazi forsake the Glory of God?

____

____

____

3. What did Gehazi do with his ill-gotten gain?

____

____

____

4. Why was the judgement on Gehazi so harsh?

____

____

____

5. Why are the ungodly without excuse in Romans 1:18-21?

____

____

____

DOUBLE PORTION
The Miracles Of Elisha

Lesson Ten

Swimming Lessons

Elisha was a prophet with a servant's heart. One moment he is going into the woods with his students to help them build larger quarters and the next he is doing battle with the whole Syrian Empire. Not every battlefront is the same and sometimes we will have multiple battles going on in a very short period of time. 2 Corinthians 4:7-18 *"But we have this treasure in earthen vessels, that the excellency of the power may be of God, and not of us. We are troubled on every side, yet not distressed; we are perplexed, but not in despair; Persecuted, but not forsaken; cast down, but not destroyed; Always bearing about in the body the dying of the Lord Jesus, that the life also of Jesus might be made manifest in our body. For we which live are alway delivered unto death for Jesus' sake, that the life also of Jesus might be made manifest in our mortal flesh. So then death worketh in us, but life in you. We having the same spirit of faith, according as it is written, I believed, and therefore have I spoken; we also believe, and therefore speak; Knowing that he which raised up the Lord Jesus shall raise up us also by Jesus, and shall present us with you. For all things are for your sakes, that the abundant grace might through the thanksgiving of many redound to the glory of God. For which cause we faint not; but though our outward man perish, yet the inward man is renewed day by day. For our light affliction, which is but for a moment, worketh for us a far more exceeding and eternal weight of glory; While we look not at the things which are seen, but at the things which are not seen: for the things which are seen are temporal; but the things which are not seen are eternal."* Elisha did not allow his fame and position to desensitize him to the needs of the common man. It is sad to see those who have lost sight of the Kingdom of God and can only focus on building a kingdom or a name for themselves. Elisha was not too important to get his hands dirty. He also never missed an opportunity to teach his students about the ways of God. If all we ever talk about is the things of this ole temporal world, then we need to lay aside those weights and begin to allow Jesus to be manifest in us. Let us refocus on Jesus and mortify the desires and passions of the flesh. Your heart is the holder of your treasures and it is out of the abundance of the heart the mouth speaketh. The more we value the Word of the Lord, the more we will speak about it in our daily life.

Scripture Text

2 Kings 6:1-7 *"And the sons of the prophets said unto Elisha, Behold now, the place where we dwell with thee is too strait for us. 2 Let us go, we pray thee, unto Jordan, and take thence every man a beam, and let us make us a place there, where we may dwell. And he answered, Go ye. 3 And one said, Be content, I pray thee, and go with thy servants. And he answered, I will go. 4 So he went with them. And when they came to Jordan, they cut down wood. 5 But as one was felling a beam, the axe head fell into the water: and he cried, and said, Alas, master! for it was borrowed. 6 And the man of God said, Where fell it? And he shewed him the place. And he cut down a stick, and cast it in thither; and the iron did swim. 7 Therefore said he, Take it up to thee. And he put out his hand, and took it."*

2 Kings 6:8-23 *"Then the king of Syria warred against Israel, and took counsel with his servants, saying, In such and such a place shall be my camp. 9 And the man of God sent unto the king of Israel, saying, Beware that thou pass not such a place; for thither the Syrians are come down. 10 And the king of Israel sent to the place which the man of God told him and warned him of, and saved himself there, not once nor twice. 11 Therefore the heart of the king of Syria was sore troubled for this thing; and he called his servants, and said unto them, Will ye not shew me which of us is for the king of Israel? 12 And one of his servants said, None,*

my lord, O king: but Elisha, the prophet that is in Israel, telleth the king of Israel the words that thou speakest in thy bedchamber. 13 And he said, Go and spy where he is, that I may send and fetch him. And it was told him, saying, Behold, he is in Dothan. 14 Therefore sent he thither horses, and chariots, and a great host: and they came by night, and compassed the city about. 15 And when the servant of the man of God was risen early, and gone forth, behold, an host compassed the city both with horses and chariots. And his servant said unto him, Alas, my master! how shall we do? 16 And he answered, Fear not: for they that be with us are more than they that be with them. 17 And Elisha prayed, and said, LORD, I pray thee, open his eyes, that he may see. And the LORD opened the eyes of the young man; and he saw: and, behold, the mountain was full of horses and chariots of fire round about Elisha. 18 And when they came down to him, Elisha prayed unto the LORD, and said, Smite this people, I pray thee, with blindness. And he smote them with blindness according to the word of Elisha. 19 And Elisha said unto them, This is not the way, neither is this the city: follow me, and I will bring you to the man whom ye seek. But he led them to Samaria. 20 And it came to pass, when they were come into Samaria, that Elisha said, LORD, open the eyes of these men, that they may see. And the LORD opened their eyes, and they saw; and, behold, they were in the midst of Samaria. 21 And the king of Israel said unto Elisha, when he saw them, My father, shall I smite them? shall I smite them? 22 And he answered, Thou shalt not smite them: wouldest thou smite those whom thou hast taken captive with thy sword and with thy bow? set bread and water before them, that they may eat and drink, and go to their master. 23 And he prepared great provision for them: and when they had eaten and drunk, he sent them away, and they went to their master. So the bands of Syria came no more into the land of Israel."

Part One

The School Of The Prophets Overflows

> 2 Kings 6:1-2 *"And the sons of the prophets said unto Elisha, Behold now, the place where we dwell with thee is too strait for us. Let us go, we pray thee, unto Jordan, and take thence every man a beam, and let us make us a place there, where we may dwell. And he answered, Go ye."*

Elisha devoted a lot of his time and resources to teaching and mentoring the Bible students at the Schools of the Prophets. Under the attentive leadership of Elisha the school had thrived and there was a great increase in students. Now the building was too small to adequately accommodate the student body. Rather than just gripe and complain about the situation, the student leaders came up with a realistic plan on how they could solve the problem and then they presented it to Elisha. They did not expect other to shower them with luxury and ease but were willing to go out and work to see the needs of the church provided for. They did not have bloated egos or haughty attitudes and declare they were too important to do common labor. The rewards in heaven will be great for all those who have worked so hard to help raise money to make church payment, pay the utility bills, buy Sunday School and Bible study material, make church bus and van payments, send youth to meetings, host camps and conferences, give to home missions, support missionaries and help the poor.

In contrast to Gehazi who took things into his own hands in order to get what he wanted, we find the student here going to the man of God and asking permission. How much better off we would be in our lives if we would consult the man of God rather than accepting secular counsel. 1 Corinthians 3:16-21 *"Know ye not that ye are the temple of God, and that the Spirit of God dwelleth in you? If any man defile the temple of God, him shall God destroy; for the temple of God is holy, which temple ye are. Let no man deceive himself. If any man among you seemeth to be wise in this world, let him become a fool, that he may be wise. For the wisdom of this world is foolishness with God. For it is written, He taketh the wise in their own craftiness. And again, The Lord knoweth the thoughts of the wise, that they are vain. Therefore let no man glory in men. For all things are yours."*

Elisha was not a proud and haughty man but was a good leader. He was able to recognize and accept a good idea from someone else and help them carry it out. We have many in our world today who think they are far superior thinkers and will not listen to the ideas of others. It is a wonderful day indeed when a church can grow to the point where they can appoint deacons to help the Pastor with the day to day administrations of the church. Acts 6:1-7 *"And in those days, when the number of the disciples was multiplied, there arose a murmuring of the Grecians against the Hebrews, because their widows were neglected in the daily ministration. Then the twelve called the multitude of the disciples unto them, and said, It is not reason that we should leave the word of God, and serve tables. Wherefore, brethren, look ye out among you seven men of honest report, full of the Holy Ghost and wisdom, whom we may appoint over this business. But we will give ourselves continually to prayer, and to the ministry of the word. And the saying pleased the whole multitude: and they chose Stephen, a man full of faith and of the Holy Ghost, and Philip, and Prochorus, and Nicanor, and Timon, and Parmenas, and Nicolas a proselyte of Antioch: Whom they set before the apostles: and when they had prayed, they laid their hands on them. And the word of God increased; and the number of the disciples multiplied in Jerusalem greatly; and a great company of the priests were obedient to the faith."* Do not desire the office of a deacon unless you are willing to work hard and give many hours of your time to the work of the Lord.

Flying Off The Handle

> 2 Kings 6:3-5 *"And one said, Be content, I pray thee, and go with thy servants. And he answered, I will go. So he went with them. And when they came to Jordan, they cut down wood. But as one was felling a beam, the axe head fell into the water: and he cried, and said, Alas, master! for it was borrowed.*

Suddenly an unforeseen events happens that causes one of the students to panic. It does not matter what the situation may be, it is always appropriate to call on the name of Jesus. We do not look at Jesus as our spare tire but he is our go to man. We go to him in prayer in the good times and in the bad times. Romans 8:35 -39 *"Who shall separate us from the love of Christ? shall tribulation, or distress, or persecution, or famine, or nakedness, or peril, or sword? As it is written, For thy sake we are killed all the day long; we are accounted as sheep for the slaughter. Nay, in all these things we are more than conquerors through him that loved us. For I am persuaded, that neither death, nor life, nor angels, nor principalities, nor powers, nor things present, nor things to come, Nor height, nor depth, nor any other creature, shall be able to separate us from the love of God, which is in Christ Jesus our Lord."* Many forget about Jesus during the good times and expect him to be there when things get ruff. It does not work that way, when you walk away from Jesus, he is not there in your time of need and you must go and seek him. Do you think Jesus is going to go with you to the clubs? When you fall in love with Jesus, nothing can separate you from His love.

Why did it fly off the handle? Did he not maintain his equipment? Did he lose the ax head because it was dull? Did he forget to bring a whet stone? Ecclesiastes 10:10 *"If the iron be blunt, and he do not whet the edge, then must he put to more strength: but wisdom is profitable to direct."* How many time have you found yourself in a mess of your own making? Many times that happens because our tongue flies off the handle. James 3:2-10 *"For in many things we offend all. If any man offend not in word, the same is a perfect man, and able also to bridle the whole body. Behold, we put bits in the horses' mouths, that they may obey us; and we turn about their whole body. Behold also the ships, which though they be so great, and are driven of fierce winds, yet are they turned about with a very small helm, whithersoever the governor listeth. Even so the tongue is a little member, and boasteth great things. Behold, how great a matter a little fire kindleth! And the tongue is a fire, a world of iniquity: so is the tongue among our members, that it defileth the whole body, and setteth on fire the course of nature; and it is set on fire of hell. For every kind of beasts, and of birds, and of serpents, and of things in the sea, is tamed, and hath been tamed of mankind: But the tongue can no man tame; it is an unruly evil, full of deadly poison. Therewith bless we God, even the Father; and therewith curse we men, which are made after the similitude of God. Out of the same mouth proceedeth blessing and cursing. My brethren, these things ought not so to be."* Using God given forethought, principles, and talents mixed with prayer and Bible study in our daily lifestyle will give us victory.

The Restoration

2 Kings 6:6-7 *"And the man of God said, Where fell it? And he shewed him the place. And he cut down a stick, and cast it in thither; and the iron did swim. 7 Therefore said he, Take it up to thee. And he put out his hand, and took it."*

The properties of iron make it sink while the properties in wood cause it to float. Was the wood giving the iron swimming lessons? (TIC) Let us allow this tragedy recorded here encourage us to believe that Jesus has the power to restore unto us every blessing that we have ever lost. Circumstances can come in and rob us of peace and joy but Jesus is the restoration and the life. Where you are at in life in not permanent. Psalms 37:3-8 *"Trust in the LORD, and do good; so shalt thou dwell in the land, and verily thou shalt be fed. Delight thyself also in the LORD; and he shall give thee the desires of thine heart. Commit thy way unto the LORD; trust also in him; and he shall bring it to pass. And he shall bring forth thy righteousness as the light, and thy judgment as the noonday. Rest in the LORD, and wait patiently for him: fret not thyself because of him who prospereth in his way, because of the man who bringeth wicked devices to pass. Cease from anger, and forsake wrath: fret not thyself in any wise to do evil."* Live for God with a whole heart and you will see the Glory of God revealed in your life.

Just like Elisha threw the branch into the water, Jesus is the righteous branch that descended from King David. Jeremiah 23:5-6 *"Behold, the days come, saith the LORD, that I will raise unto David a righteous Branch, and a King shall reign and prosper, and shall execute judgment and justice in the earth. In his days Judah shall be saved, and Israel shall dwell safely: and this is his name whereby he shall be called, THE LORD OUR RIGHTEOUSNESS."* Jesus was cut down and placed in the tomb. Just like He rose out of the ground, when we receive the Holy Ghost, the righteous branch raises us out of the miry clay. We are the iron that sunk in the miry clay and Jesus is the branch that raised us up and out of it. Psalms 40:2 *"He brought me up also out of an horrible pit, out of the miry clay, and set my feet upon a rock, and established my goings."* The name of Jesus has all power.

Let us look at another miracle where God caused something to float on the water. Matthew 14:25-31 *"And in the fourth watch of the night Jesus went unto them, walking on the sea. And when the disciples saw him walking on the sea, they were troubled, saying, It is a spirit; and they cried out for fear. But straightway Jesus spake unto them, saying, Be of good cheer; it is I; be not afraid. And Peter answered him and said, Lord, if it be thou, bid me come unto thee on the water. And he said, Come. And when Peter was come down out of the ship, he walked on the water, to go to Jesus. But when he saw the wind boisterous, he was afraid; and beginning to sink, he cried, saying, Lord, save me. And immediately Jesus stretched forth his hand, and caught him, and said unto him, O thou of little faith, wherefore didst thou doubt?"*

We also see where Elisha put out his hand and took up the sinking iron (man). We are going to find ourselves at times where the storms of life will overcome us and we will need the man of God to put out his hand and pull us to safety.

Part Two

No Privacy In The Bedchamber

> 2 Kings 6:8-12 "*Then the king of Syria warred against Israel, and took counsel with his servants, saying, In such and such a place shall be my camp. 9 And the man of God sent unto the king of Israel, saying, Beware that thou pass not such a place; for thither the Syrians are come down. 10 And the king of Israel sent to the place which the man of God told him and warned him of, and saved himself there, not once nor twice. 11 Therefore the heart of the king of Syria was sore troubled for this thing; and he called his servants, and said unto them, Will ye not shew me which of us is for the king of Israel? 12 And one of his servants said, None, my lord, O king: but Elisha, the prophet that is in Israel, telleth the king of Israel the words that thou speakest in thy bedchamber.*"

The king of Syria was a very wicked person. He had not one once of gratitude in his heart for what God had done for his Captain Naaman. It is only a wicked heart that will return evil for good. There is no indication that Israel had done anything to provoke King Benhadad. Plus it did not make sense considering the defeat he had suffered early (1 Kings 20:1-34). Many today quickly forget what God has done for them and run greedily after carnal gain. James 5:1-5 "*Go to now, ye rich men, weep and howl for your miseries that shall come upon you. Your riches are corrupted, and your garments are motheaten. Your gold and silver is cankered; and the rust of them shall be a witness against you, and shall eat your flesh as it were fire. Ye have heaped treasure together for the last days. Behold, the hire of the labourers who have reaped down your fields, which is of you kept back by fraud, crieth: and the cries of them which have reaped are entered into the ears of the Lord of sabaoth. Ye have lived in pleasure on the earth, and been wanton; ye have nourished your hearts, as in a day of slaughter.*" We need to remember that we will be blessed when we put God first.

We see a prophet with grace and honor stepping out of the back woods into the palace to do the work of the Lord after proving that he could not be bought with money earlier. King Benhadad had a plan to ambush the king of Israel. King Benhadad had obtained information about the normal travel plans of the king of Israel and set a trap to catch him. Elisha sends a messenger to warn King Jehoram of the trap that had been set for him. Once again King Jehoram does not believe the prophet, so he sends spies to check out the ambush. To his amazement the prophet was correct not just once but on multiple occasions about the traps. Even today the bad habits of man is still getting him into trouble. We go down the same paths and do the same things over and over thinking we will not get caught or will not have to pay the consequences this time. 2 Timothy 2:19-26 *"Nevertheless the foundation of God standeth sure, having this seal, The Lord knoweth them that are his. And, Let every one that nameth the name of Christ depart from iniquity. But in a great house there are not only vessels of gold and of silver, but also of wood and of earth; and some to honour, and some to dishonour. If a man therefore purge himself from these, he shall be a vessel unto honour, sanctified, and meet for the master's use, and prepared unto every good work. Flee also youthful lusts: but follow righteousness, faith, charity, peace, with them that call on the Lord out of a pure heart. But foolish and unlearned questions avoid, knowing that they do gender strifes. And the servant of the Lord must not strive; but be gentle unto all men, apt to teach, patient, In meekness instructing those that oppose themselves; if God peradventure will give them repentance to the acknowledging of the truth; And that they may recover themselves out of the snare of the devil, who are taken captive by him at his will."* Many people blame their failure on the devil, while all along they knew the trap was there and walked right into it anyway. It is time to find an altar and surrender all the kingdoms of our heart to Jesus. This constant circle of stumbling and crawling to the altar to just get up and do it all over again must be broken. When we clean all the world out of our lives then the man of God can speak a warning unto and we will head it. Allow the man of God to put some guardrails (holiness standards) in your life so you won't go down those wrong paths anymore. The reason those guardrails are there is because someone went off the road there and lost their life. The reason your Pastor preaches holiness standards is because someone got to close to the world and lost their soul there. Proverbs 7:5-27 *"That they may keep thee from the strange woman, from the stranger which flattereth with her words. For at the window of my house I looked through my casement, And beheld among the simple ones, I discerned among the youths, a young man void of understanding, Passing through the street near her corner; and he went the way to her house, In the twilight, in the evening, in the black and dark night: And, behold, there met him a woman with the attire of an harlot, and subtil of heart. (She is loud and stubborn; her feet abide not in her house: Now is she without, now in the streets, and lieth in wait at every corner.) So she caught him, and kissed him, and with an impudent face said unto him, I have peace offerings with me; this day have I payed my vows. Therefore came I forth to meet thee, diligently to seek thy face, and I have found thee. I have decked my bed with coverings of tapestry, with carved works, with fine linen of Egypt. I have perfumed my bed with myrrh, aloes, and cinnamon. Come, let us take our fill of love until the morning: let us solace ourselves with loves. For the goodman is not at home, he is gone a long journey: He hath taken a bag of money with him, and will come home at the day appointed. With her much fair speech she caused him to yield, with the flattering of her lips she forced him. He goeth after her straightway, as an ox goeth to the slaughter, or as a fool to the correction of the stocks; Till a dart strike through his liver; as a bird hasteth to the snare, and knoweth not that it is for his life. Hearken unto me now therefore, O ye children, and attend to the words of my mouth. Let not thine heart decline to her ways, go not astray in her paths. For she hath cast down many wounded: yea, many strong men have been slain by her. Her house is the way to hell, going down to the chambers of death."*

King Benhadad was so far from God that he never imagined that the prophet was the source of King Jehoram information. So he begin to look for a traitor in his own ranks. It was then that he came face to face with the revelation that the prophet of God had intimate details of his every word and action. How foolish it is for man to think that we can hide from God. Adam and Eve tried it and how did that turn out? We are so much better off to confess and change our ways than to hide and justify our sins. Hebrews 4:12-13 *"For the word of God is quick, and powerful, and sharper than any twoedged sword, piercing even to the dividing asunder of soul and spirit, and of the joints and marrow, and is a discerner of the thoughts and intents of the heart. Neither is there any creature that is not manifest in his sight: but all things are naked and opened unto the eyes of him with whom we have to do."*

Elisha Got His Chariots Of Fire

2 Kings 6:13-17 "And he said, Go and spy where he is, that I may send and fetch him. And it was told him, saying, Behold, he is in Dothan. 14 Therefore sent he thither horses, and chariots, and a great host: and they came by night, and compassed the city about. 15 And when the servant of the man of God was risen early, and gone forth, behold, an host compassed the city both with horses and chariots. And his servant said unto him, Alas, my master! how shall we do? 16 And he answered, Fear not: for they that be with us are more than they that be with them. 17 And Elisha prayed, and said, LORD, I pray thee, open his eyes, that he may see. And the LORD opened the eyes of the young man; and he saw: and, behold, the mountain was full of horses and chariots of fire round about Elisha."

King Benhadad had a hard heart just like Pharaoh. His actions demonstrate that he thought he could fight against God and win. He was using his education, intelligence, wealth, power and authority to silence the man of God. The world we live in today is in an all-out war to silence the man of God. The battle is good versus evil. The jargon that is used and the stage it is set on is all camouflage to hide the true agenda of hell. No longer is it a battle to force us to tolerate evil. It is a battle where evil is promoted on ever hand and voice of truth is being snuffed out. It has been a gradual process where God has been removed from ever facet of society and has been replace with perversion. 2 Timothy 3:1-17 *"This know also, that in the last days perilous times shall come. For men shall be lovers of their own selves, covetous, boasters, proud, blasphemers, disobedient to parents, unthankful, unholy, Without natural affection, trucebreakers, false accusers, incontinent, fierce, despisers of those that are good, Traitors, heady, highminded, lovers of pleasures more than lovers of God; Having a form of godliness, but denying the power thereof: from such turn away. For of this sort are they which creep into houses, and lead captive silly women laden with sins, led away with divers lusts, Ever learning, and never able to come to the knowledge of the truth. Now as Jannes and Jambres withstood Moses, so do these also resist the truth: men of corrupt minds, reprobate concerning the faith. But they shall proceed no further: for their folly shall be manifest unto all men, as theirs also was. But thou hast fully known my doctrine, manner of life, purpose, faith, longsuffering, charity, patience, Persecutions, afflictions, which came unto me at Antioch, at Iconium, at Lystra; what persecutions I endured: but out of them all the Lord delivered me. Yea, and all that will live godly in Christ Jesus shall suffer persecution. But evil men and seducers shall wax worse and worse, deceiving, and being deceived. But continue thou in the things which thou hast learned and hast been assured of, knowing of whom thou hast learned them; And that from a child thou hast known the holy scriptures, which are able to make thee wise unto salvation through faith which is in Christ Jesus. All scripture is given by inspiration of God, and is profitable for doctrine, for reproof, for correction, for instruction in righteousness: That the man of God may be perfect, throughly furnished unto all good works."*

Dothan is where this miracle occurred at. The word Dothan means "double feast" and is located west of the Jordan River in the northeast part of Samaria. King Benhadad was trying to be smart and crafty by sending a sizeable force to capture one prophet. He thought Elisha had some power but was no match for the mighty King Benhadad. It is amazing how so many pay lip service to God but continue to live in sin not believing in the judgements of God. As long as they are moving forward and God has not struck them down yet, they think they are getting by with their sins. 1 Peter 4:17-18 *"For the time is come that judgment must begin at the house of God: and if it first begin at us, what shall the end be of them that obey not the gospel of God? And if the righteous scarcely be saved, where shall the ungodly and the sinner appear?"* I find it very interesting that he makes a distinction between the ungodly and the sinner but makes it very clear that both of them will be lost.

Gehazi had been replaced and the honeymoon for the new servant was over. The enemy had come against them and the new servant had no clue what to do. As we start our walk with God, we can be overwhelmed sometimes by the battles of the flesh versus the Spirit. Just as Elisha had that steady voice of faith to speak into his servant heart, the child of God today needs the steady voice of faith that his Pastor speaks into his heart. It is during those times of trials that we need the man of God to have a word that will open our eyes to the Spirit world. Hebrews 1:13-14 *"But to which of the angels said he at any time, Sit on my right hand, until I make thine enemies thy footstool? Are they not all ministering spirits, sent forth to minister for them who shall be heirs of salvation?"* Let us not be consumed with the enemies that we can see, all the while forgetting about the warriors that are on our side (Luke 2:13). Jesus talks about the angels that he could call down to fight for him. Matthew 26:53 *"Thinkest thou that I cannot now pray to my Father, and he shall presently give me more than twelve legions of angels?"* You are never alone, God is always ready to help you fight your battle. All we need to do is call on the name of Jesus and we have access to all the power of heaven and earth.

Ministering Healing To Our Enemies

2 Kings 6:18-23 *"And when they came down to him, Elisha prayed unto the LORD, and said, Smite this people, I pray thee, with blindness. And he smote them with blindness according to the word of Elisha. 19 And Elisha said unto them, This is not the way, neither is this the city: follow me, and I will bring you to the man whom ye seek. But he led them to Samaria. 20 And it came to pass, when they were come into Samaria, that Elisha said, LORD, open the eyes of these men, that they may see. And the LORD opened their eyes, and they saw; and, behold, they were in the midst of Samaria. 21 And the king of Israel said unto Elisha, when he saw them, My father, shall I smite them? shall I smite them? 22 And he answered, Thou shalt not smite them: wouldest thou smite those whom thou hast taken captive with thy sword and with thy bow? set bread and water before them, that they may eat and drink, and go to their master. 23 And he prepared great provision for them: and when they had eaten and drunk, he sent them away, and they went to their master. So the bands of Syria came no more into the land of Israel."*

The prayers of Elisha were answered once again and the soldiers were smitten with blindness. He was then able to lead them where the Lord wanted them to be. It is not till people realize that they are lost, that you are able to lead them to truth so that they can be saved from sin. 2 Corinthians 4:2-6 *"But have renounced the hidden things of dishonesty, not walking in craftiness, nor handling the word of God deceitfully; but by manifestation of the truth commending ourselves to every man's conscience in the sight of God. But if our gospel be hid, it is hid to them that are lost: In whom the god of this world hath blinded the minds of them which believe not, lest the light of the glorious gospel of Christ, who is the image of God, should shine unto them. For we preach not ourselves, but Christ Jesus the Lord; and ourselves your servants for Jesus' sake. For God, who commanded the light to shine out of darkness, hath shined in our hearts, to give the light of the knowledge of the glory of God in the face of Jesus Christ."*

You think the servant of Elisha was amazed, just think how amazed King Jehoram was when Elisha marched in with the Syrian army. King Jehoram tune is changed and he show lots of respect for Elisha even calling him "father." How many times is the church surprised when God moves? We should never take the move of God for granted, but we should always come to church expecting a move of God. 1 Corinthians 2:1-5 *"And I, brethren, when I came to you, came not with excellency of speech or of wisdom, declaring unto you the testimony of God. For I determined not to know any thing among you, save Jesus Christ, and him crucified. And I was with you in weakness, and in fear, and in much trembling. And my speech and my preaching was not with enticing words of man's wisdom, but in demonstration of the Spirit and of power: That your faith should not stand in the wisdom of men, but in the power of God."* It is not the fact that God did not show up when we have a dead service, it is the fact that we did not respond to the moving of the Holy Ghost that produces a dead service.

So many don't know what to do when they see their enemy in trouble. The king of Israel thought rubbing their faces in the dirt would solve his problems with Syria. It was kindness and love that God used to bring a season of peace with Syria. 1 Corinthians 13:1-7 *"Though I speak with the tongues of men and of angels, and have not charity, I am become as sounding brass, or a tinkling cymbal. And though I have the gift of prophecy, and understand all mysteries, and all knowledge; and though I have all faith, so that I could remove mountains, and have not charity, I am nothing. And though I bestow all my goods to feed the poor, and though I give my body to be burned, and have not charity, it profiteth me nothing. Charity suffereth long, and is kind; charity envieth not; charity vaunteth not itself, is not puffed up, Doth not behave itself unseemly, seeketh not her own, is not easily provoked, thinketh no evil; Rejoiceth not in iniquity, but rejoiceth in the truth; Beareth all things, believeth all things, hopeth all things, endureth all things."* Carnal responses will never bring Spiritual results. Many times those harsh word people have said to you was the results of the hurt that was in their soul. We need to rise above our feeling and reach out to our enemies when they begin to see the light. Paul was on the road to Damascus when he saw the light. Acts 9:3-6 *"And as he journeyed, he came near Damascus: and suddenly there shined round about him a light from heaven: And he fell to the earth, and heard a voice saying unto him, Saul, Saul, why persecutest thou me? And he said, Who art thou, Lord? And the Lord said, I am Jesus whom thou persecutest: it is hard for thee to kick against the pricks. And he trembling and astonished said, Lord, what wilt thou have me to do? And the Lord said unto him, Arise, and go into the city, and it shall be told thee what thou must do."* Ananias and many other ministers had to rise above their feelings and show kindness and love unto Paul so that he might do the work of the Lord. Just like Paul had to have someone show him what he must do, we are not going to make it to heaven without a Pastor to preach to us.

Discussion Questions

1.   What does temporal mean?

____

____

____

2.   Why were they cutting down trees?

____

____

____

3.   Why do we fly off the handle?

____

____

____

4.   What does blindness represent?

____

____

____

5.   What is wrong with carnal responses?

____

____

____

DOUBLE PORTION
The Miracles Of Elisha

Lesson Eleven

The Windows Of Heaven

What a bleak and deprived state of existence that sin had brought the nation of Israel to. God had sent droughts and famines over and over to bring them to their knees. Like a child who refused to correct his wrong doing they were reaping the bitter dregs of disobedience. How easy It would have been for them to forsake to source of all their suffering and return to the river of blessings. But like many today they were too caught up in being a part of the world around them and refusing to acknowledge that the world was their source of destruction.   I know that it sounds crazy and revolutionary to the carnal mind, but we are called to come out of the world.   2 Corinthians 6:14-18 *"Be ye not unequally yoked together with unbelievers: for what fellowship hath righteousness with unrighteousness? and what communion hath light with darkness? And what concord hath Christ with Belial? or what part hath he that believeth with an infidel? And what agreement hath the temple of God with idols? for ye are the temple of the living God; as God hath said, I will dwell in them, and walk in them; and I will be their God, and they shall be my people. Wherefore come out from among them, and be ye separate, saith the Lord, and touch not the unclean thing; and I will receive you, And will be a Father unto you, and ye shall be my sons and daughters, saith the*

Lord Almighty." The people of God has always been different from the world. There is still great pressure in our world today to conform to the values, ideas, and idols of the world. Romans 12:1-2 *"I beseech you therefore, brethren, by the mercies of God, that ye present your bodies a living sacrifice, holy, acceptable unto God, which is your reasonable service. And be not conformed to this world: but be ye transformed by the renewing of your mind, that ye may prove what is that good, and acceptable, and perfect, will of God."* It is only through the power of the Holy Ghost that we will ever be able to overcome the world.

It was not a large army that defeated the Syrians. It was four men who made up their minds they were not going to sit there until they died. God used four rejects to open the windows of heaven. How long are you going to sit on your miracle? It does not take an army to begin a revolution. All it takes is a few men that are willing to take a stand. It does not take a large church to have revival. All it takes is a few believers who are willing to pray and work until God moves. 2 Corinthians 10:3-5 *"For though we walk in the flesh, we do not war after the flesh: (For the weapons of our warfare are not carnal, but mighty through God to the pulling down of strong holds;) Casting down imaginations, and every high thing that exalteth itself against the knowledge of God, and bringing into captivity every thought to the obedience of Christ."* Those impossible to conquer strongholds in your city will come down when you begin to battle on your knees. Many times the greatest battle of the week is to get to pre service prayer at church. Shame on you if you can make the gospel singings and skip prayer time and prayer meetings. Until there is fire in the prayer room there will never be fire in the worship. It is when God is being lifted up that men will be drawn to him. Psalms 42:1-4 *"As the hart panteth after the water brooks, so panteth my soul after thee, O God. My soul thirsteth for God, for the living God: when shall I come and appear before God? My tears have been my meat day and night, while they continually say unto me, Where is thy God? When I remember these things, I pour out my soul in me: for I had gone with the multitude, I went with them to the house of God, with the voice of joy and praise, with a multitude that kept holyday."* Let us be thirsty for revival.

Scripture Text

2 Kings 6:24-33 *"And it came to pass after this, that Benhadad*

king of Syria gathered all his host, and went up, and besieged Samaria. 25 And there was a great famine in Samaria: and, behold, they besieged it, until an ass's head was sold for fourscore pieces of silver, and the fourth part of a cab of dove's dung for five pieces of silver. 26 And as the king of Israel was passing by upon the wall, there cried a woman unto him, saying, Help, my lord, O king. 27 And he said, If the LORD do not help thee, whence shall I help thee? out of the barnfloor, or out of the winepress? 28 And the king said unto her, What aileth thee? And she answered, This woman said unto me, Give thy son, that we may eat him to day, and we will eat my son to morrow. 29 So we boiled my son, and did eat him: and I said unto her on the next day, Give thy son, that we may eat him: and she hath hid her son. 30 And it came to pass, when the king heard the words of the woman, that he rent his clothes; and he passed by upon the wall, and the people looked, and, behold, he had sackcloth within upon his flesh. 31 Then he said, God do so and more also to me, if the head of Elisha the son of Shaphat shall stand on him this day. 32 But Elisha sat in his house, and the elders sat with him; and the king sent a man from before him: but ere the messenger came to him, he said to the elders, See ye how this son of a murderer hath sent to take away mine head? look, when the messenger cometh, shut the door, and hold him fast at the door: is not the sound of his master's feet behind him? 33 And while he yet talked with them, behold, the messenger came down unto him: and he said, Behold, this evil is of the LORD; what should I wait for the LORD any longer?"

2 Kings 7:1-20 *"Then Elisha said, Hear ye the word of the LORD; Thus saith the LORD, To morrow about this time shall a measure of fine flour be sold for a shekel, and two measures of barley for a shekel, in the gate of Samaria. 2 Then a lord on whose hand the king leaned answered the man of God, and said, Behold, if the LORD would make windows in heaven, might this thing be? And he said, Behold, thou shalt see it with thine eyes, but shalt not eat thereof. 3 And there were four leprous men at the entering in of the gate: and they said one to another, Why sit we here until we die? 4 If we say, We will enter into the city, then the famine is in the city, and we shall die there: and if we sit still here, we die also. Now therefore come, and let us fall unto the host of the Syrians: if they save us alive, we shall live; and if they kill us, we shall but die. 5 And they rose up in the twilight, to go unto the camp of the Syrians: and when they were come to the uttermost part of the*

camp of Syria, behold, there was no man there. 6 For the Lord had made the host of the Syrians to hear a noise of chariots, and a noise of horses, even the noise of a great host: and they said one to another, Lo, the king of Israel hath hired against us the kings of the Hittites, and the kings of the Egyptians, to come upon us. 7 Wherefore they arose and fled in the twilight, and left their tents, and their horses, and their asses, even the camp as it was, and fled for their life. 8 And when these lepers came to the uttermost part of the camp, they went into one tent, and did eat and drink, and carried thence silver, and gold, and raiment, and went and hid it; and came again, and entered into another tent, and carried thence also, and went and hid it. 9 Then they said one to another, We do not well: this day is a day of good tidings, and we hold our peace: if we tarry till the morning light, some mischief will come upon us: now therefore come, that we may go and tell the king's household. 10 So they came and called unto the porter of the city: and they told them, saying, We came to the camp of the Syrians, and, behold, there was no man there, neither voice of man, but horses tied, and asses tied, and the tents as they were. 11 And he called the porters; and they told it to the king's house within. 12 And the king arose in the night, and said unto his servants, I will now shew you what the Syrians have done to us. They know that we be hungry; therefore are they gone out of the camp to hide themselves in the field, saying, When they come out of the city, we shall catch them alive, and get into the city. 13 And one of his servants answered and said, Let some take, I pray thee, five of the horses that remain, which are left in the city, (behold, they are as all the multitude of Israel that are left in it: behold, I say, they are even as all the multitude of the Israelites that are consumed:) and let us send and see. 14 They took therefore two chariot horses; and the king sent after the host of the Syrians, saying, Go and see. 15 And they went after them unto Jordan: and, lo, all the way was full of garments and vessels, which the Syrians had cast away in their haste. And the messengers returned, and told the king. 16 And the people went out, and spoiled the tents of the Syrians. So a measure of fine flour was sold for a shekel, and two measures of barley for a shekel, according to the word of the LORD. 17 And the king appointed the lord on whose hand he leaned to have the charge of the gate: and the people trode upon him in the gate, and he died, as the man of God had said, who spake when the king came down to him. 18 And it came to pass as the man of God had spoken to the king, saying, Two measures of barley for a shekel, *and a measure of fine flour for a shekel, shall be to morrow about this time in the gate of Samaria: 19 And that lord answered the man of God, and said, Now, behold, if the LORD should make windows in heaven, might such a thing be? And he said, Behold, thou shalt see it with thine eyes, but shalt not eat thereof. 20 And so it fell out unto him: for the people trode upon him in the gate, and he died."*

From Bad To Worst

2 Kings 6:24-30 "*And it came to pass after this, that Benhadad king of Syria gathered all his host, and went up, and besieged Samaria. 25 And there was a great famine in Samaria: and, behold, they besieged it, until an ass's head was sold for fourscore pieces of silver, and the fourth part of a cab of dove's dung for five pieces of silver. 26 And as the king of Israel was passing by upon the wall, there cried a woman unto him, saying, Help, my lord, O king. 27 And he said, If the LORD do not help thee, whence shall I help thee? out of the barnfloor, or out of the winepress? 28 And the king said unto her, What aileth thee? And she answered, This woman said unto me, Give thy son, that we may eat him to day, and we will eat my son to morrow. 29 So we boiled my son, and did eat him: and I said unto her on the next day, Give thy son, that we may eat him: and she hath hid her son. 30 And it came to pass, when the king heard the words of the woman, that he rent his clothes; and he passed by upon the wall, and the people looked, and, behold, he had sackcloth within upon his flesh*"

How low into the miry clay mankind can sink when he is in the clutches of sin. The nation of Israel had never recovered from the blithe of sin that King Ahab and Queen Jezebel had infected every corner of the country with. The curse of sin had brought pain and misery time and time again. The country had been under a curse of famine for quite some time and that within itself had made for very dire times. Now the powerful empire of Syria put a military blockade around Samaria not allowing any aid or trade to come into Samaria. This makes a bad situation a lot worst. Let us try to get a grip on how bad the situation was. Even today someone must be desperate to eat the head of a beast of burden. The curious part is the mention of the selling of a cab of dove's dung. Cab: A Hebrew measurement, the sixth part of a seah, and the eighteenth part of an ephah. A cab contained three pints and one third, of our liquid measure, or two pints and five sixths, of our dry measure. The common name "bird's milk" or "bird's dung" is given to the bulb, Ornithogalum umbellatum which is considered an invasive noxious weed which grows in this region. The foliage and bulbs contain toxic alkaloids that will poison livestock. The cooked or roasted bulbs are reportedly edible to humans. Today, the plant is known as "Star of Bethlehem." Carl Linnaeus, the botanist, called it the "dove's dung" Ornithogalum. There are some who call other plants "dove's dung" but I find little evidence to back up their claim. Of course it could have been literal dove's dung. We also need to note that the ass is considered an unclean animal. Thus the nation of Israel was forbidden to eat it. Because of the unbridled immorality running amuck in the nation, we have people resorting to cannibalism. When you lose your morals, you have no problem committing murder. Millions of babies are murdered every year because people are trying to rid themselves of the consequences of immorality. The blood of these murdered babies are crying out from the ground. Genesis 4:8-11 *"And Cain talked with Abel his brother: and it came to pass, when they were in the field, that Cain rose up against Abel his brother, and slew him. And the LORD said unto Cain, Where is Abel thy brother? And he said, I know not: Am I my brother's keeper? And he said, What hast thou done? the voice of thy brother's blood crieth unto me from the ground. And now art thou cursed from the earth, which hath opened her mouth to receive thy brother's blood from thy hand."*

Rather than falling upon her face and calling out to the Lord, we find this lady seeking help from an ungodly king. She is asking this king to help her commit murder and other despicable acts. Man often seeks out other to help him facilitate his debase lifestyle. We should never be a part of helping someone else to sin. 1 Timothy 5:22 *"…neither be partaker of other men's sins: keep thyself pure."* Do we want to bring the curse of sin upon our heads or our household? We are also guilty when we stand idly by and refuse to speak out against sin. Ezekiel 3:17-18 *"Son of man, I have made thee a watchman unto the house of Israel: therefore hear the word at my mouth, and give them warning from me. When I say unto the wicked, Thou shalt surely die; and thou givest him not warning, nor speakest to warn the wicked from his wicked way, to save his life; the same wicked man shall die in his iniquity; but his blood will I require at thine hand."* It is another case of a mother bringing a story about two babies to the king but King Jehoram does not have the wisdom of King Solomon to solve it. Whether it was in mockery or a feeble attempt to make himself look pious, the king puts on sackcloth and parades before the people. So much of what is done in the name of religion these days is done in order to help a man build an image for himself. Society is looking for something that looks and sounds good to the carnal man, caring not that it is rotten on the inside and full of death. Matthew 23:24-28 *"Ye blind guides, which strain at a gnat, and swallow a camel. Woe unto you, scribes and Pharisees, hypocrites! for ye make clean the outside of the cup and of the platter, but within they are full of extortion and excess. Thou blind Pharisee, cleanse first that which is within the cup and platter, that the outside of them may be clean also. Woe unto you, scribes and Pharisees, hypocrites! for ye are like unto whited sepulchres, which indeed appear beautiful outward, but are within full of dead men's bones, and of all uncleanness. Even so ye also outwardly appear righteous unto men, but within ye are full of hypocrisy and iniquity."* Give me a Pastor who will preach the truth even when it rubs me the wrong way. I've got to make heaven my home and it will be cheap at any cost.

The Son Of Shaphat Or The Son Of A Murderer

> 2 Kings 6:31-33 *"Then he said, God do so and more also to me, if the head of Elisha the son of Shaphat shall stand on him this day. 32 But Elisha sat in his house, and the elders sat with him; and the king sent a man from before him: but ere the messenger came to him, he said to the elders, See ye how this son of a murderer hath sent to take away mine head? look, when the messenger cometh, shut the door, and hold him fast at the door: is not the sound of his master's feet behind him? 33 And while he yet talked with them, behold, the messenger came down unto him: and he said, Behold, this evil is of the LORD; what should I wait for the LORD any longer?"*

To kill the goose that lays the golden eggs. What a warped mind the king had developed. He was intent on killing the only hope the nation of Israel had of hearing from God or receiving deliverance from their current dilemma. It is the same mentality that wants to kill the postman for delivering bad news. Today, this spirit causes people to change churches if the preacher delivers a message from God that they don't want to hear. My friend, it is the same preacher that delivers the bad news that also can deliver the miracle that you need in order to go on living. You had better stick with a Pastor that can hear from God and not one who just wants your money. 2 Timothy 4:1-4 *"I charge thee therefore before God, and the Lord Jesus Christ, who shall judge the quick and the dead at his appearing and his kingdom; Preach the word; be instant in season, out of season; reprove, rebuke, exhort with all longsuffering and doctrine. For the time will come when they will not endure sound doctrine; but after their own lusts shall they heap to themselves teachers, having itching ears; And they shall turn away their ears from the truth, and shall be turned unto fables."* Don't be a victim of sugar coated fruity tootie preaching. It looks, smells and taste good but has nothing in it to help you weather the storms of life and will eventually turn you into a reprobate. If you ever buck the preacher in order to give your children what they want, you will soon begin to regret it all the days of your life and will never be able to undo it. Hebrews 12:5-11 *"And ye have forgotten the exhortation which speaketh unto you as unto children, My son, despise not thou the chastening of the Lord, nor faint when thou art rebuked of him: For whom the Lord loveth he chasteneth, and scourgeth every son whom he receiveth. If ye endure chastening, God dealeth with you as with sons; for what son is he whom the father chasteneth not? But if ye be without chastisement, whereof all are partakers, then are ye bastards, and not sons. Furthermore we have had fathers of our flesh which corrected us, and we gave them reverence: shall we not much rather be in subjection unto the Father of spirits, and live? For they verily for a few days chastened us after their own pleasure; but he for our profit, that we might be partakers of his holiness. Now no chastening for the present seemeth to be joyous, but grievous: nevertheless afterward it yieldeth the peaceable fruit of righteousness unto them which are exercised thereby."* What a miserable existence, to know that you helped send your own children to hell.   Don't let the perverted entertainment industry install their ungodly values into your children.   Children are very easily influenced and must be protected from evil. The major problem we have today is not bad children, it is bad parents. The children would not behave the way they do if the parents would take time to discipline and teach them the Bible way.   During Jesus' earthly ministry he showed great love and concern for children. It is a blessing to any church to have the fresh life that children bring to it.   Let us start at a young age teaching our children respect for the house of God and the man of God. The Bible tells parents to give the Pastor free course to correct and instruct their children. Then they must back up every word that he speaks to them. Without the Holy Ghost working in your children's life they are nothing but little sinners (John 8:44). You need the help of the church to raise your children in the fear of God.

King Jehoram was trying to be condescending to the Prophet Elisha by calling him the son of Shaphat. He did not realize that was the name he was anointed under. 1 Kings 19:16 *"And Jehu the son of Nimshi shalt thou anoint to be king over Israel: and Elisha the son of Shaphat of Abelmeholah shalt thou anoint to be prophet in thy room."* Don't ever sell the anointing for the acceptance of man. It is the anointing that breaks the yoke of bondage. To be able to speak the word of the Lord under the anointing is far more valuable than diamonds or rubies. But King Jehoram had no such heritage, he was the son of a murderer. His parents, King Ahab and Queen Jezebel had murdered a Godly man in order to feed their greed (1 Kings 21:1-16). What kind of heritage are you leaving your children? A preacher killer or a preacher builder.

While their world was in chaos, Elisha and the elders were gathered together in prayer for their nation. God spoke to His prophet and warned him of the danger and gave him a word for the times. There are a multiple of miracles contain within this lesson today. Elisha even predicted that the messenger of the king was coming and then the king himself. It still boggles my mind that the hypocrites think that God is going to save them out of their calamity. Proverbs 1:24-31 *"Because I have called, and ye refused; I have stretched out my hand, and no man regarded; But ye have set at nought all my counsel, and would none of my reproof: I also will laugh at your calamity; I will mock when your fear cometh; When your fear cometh as desolation, and your destruction cometh as a whirlwind; when distress and anguish cometh upon you. Then shall they call upon me, but I will not answer; they shall seek me early, but they shall not find me: For that they hated knowledge, and did not choose the fear of the LORD: They would none of my counsel: they despised all my reproof. Therefore shall they eat of the fruit of their own way, and be filled with their own devices."* You don't work for the devil and get a paycheck from the Lord. Don't give me that "you are basically a good person."   Romans 3:9-12 *"What then? are we better than they? No, in no wise: for we have before proved both Jews and Gentiles, that they are all under sin; As it is written, There is none righteous, no, not one: There is none that understandeth, there is none that seeketh after God. They are all gone out of the way, they are together become unprofitable; there is none that doeth good, no, not one."*   Until you have been born again, you have no promise of the blessings of the Lord.

Hell Can Be One Block From Calvary

> 2 Kings 7:1-2 *"Then Elisha said, Hear ye the word of the LORD; Thus saith the LORD, To morrow about this time shall a measure of fine flour be sold for a shekel, and two measures of barley for a shekel, in the gate of Samaria. 2 Then a lord on whose hand the king leaned answered the man of God, and said, Behold, if the LORD would make windows in heaven, might this thing be? And he said, Behold, thou shalt see it with thine eyes, but shalt not eat thereof.*

I will never forget the message on hell that I heard when I was a youth. The preacher told of a group of backslidden youth who pulled into the Calvary Pentecostal Church parking lot in their new sports car and begin to make fun of the preacher. They shouted at the preacher, "Hey man how far is hell from here?" In a sober prophetic voice he replied "Hell is only one block from Calvary." They gunned their motor and slung gravel as they pull out of the parking lot, laughing at the preacher as they left. In just a few moments the preacher heard the screech of brakes and the rending of metal as the boys were run over by a truck and entered into hell one block from Calvary Pentecostal Church.

Even though the prophet was foretelling of an abundance of food to come tomorrow, the lord of the king decided to mock the prophet rather than believe.   He did not realize that he was so close to deliverance that he would see it but would never again be able to taste of the goodness of the Lord.   Hebrews 12:14-17 *"Follow peace with all men, and holiness, without which no man shall see the Lord: Looking diligently lest any man fail of the grace of God; lest any root of bitterness springing up trouble you, and thereby many be defiled; Lest there be any fornicator, or profane person, as Esau, who for one morsel of meat sold his birthright. For ye know how that afterward, when he would have inherited the blessing, he was rejected: for he found no place of repentance, though he sought it carefully with tears."* I have seen more saints become bitter over holiness and lose out with God than any other sin. The enemy of our soul is constantly trying to entangle us with the lust of this world. It becomes a cycle of man rejecting, not believing and mocking God. Their immorality turns them into a profane persons who will flaunt their sin as they proclaim themselves Christians. There is a point of no return. I hope and pray that the preacher reaches them before they slip over the edge.

Who are we to limit God? Little did the lord of the king know that when God opens the windows of heaven that nothing is too big for our God. There is no ocean too deep or mountain too high to stop our God. If we could just have the faith of a grain of mustard seed. Matthew 17:20 *"And Jesus said unto them, Because of your unbelief: for verily I say unto you, If ye have faith as a grain of mustard seed, ye shall say unto this mountain, Remove hence to yonder place; and it shall remove; and nothing shall be impossible unto you."* There is nothing that can stop someone who hears from God and will just keep on going.

How Long Are You Going To Sit Here?

> 2 Kings 7:3-7 *"And there were four leprous men at the entering in of the gate: and they said one to another, Why sit we here until we die? 4 If we say, We will enter into the city, then the famine is in the city, and we shall die there: and if we sit still here, we die also. Now therefore come, and let us fall unto the host of the Syrians: if they save us alive, we shall live; and if they kill us, we shall but die. 5 And they rose up in the twilight, to go unto the camp of the Syrians: and when they were come to the uttermost part of the camp of Syria, behold, there was no man there. 6 For the Lord had made the host of the Syrians to hear a noise of chariots, and a noise of horses, even the noise of a great host: and they said one to another, Lo, the king of Israel hath hired against us the kings of the Hittites, and the kings of the Egyptians, to come upon us. 7 Wherefore they arose and fled in the twilight, and left their tents, and their horses, and their asses, even the camp as it was, and fled for their life.*

They were outcast, rejects and unable to be a part of normal society. They were lepers sitting at the gates hoping to get a few crumbs from their betters. A more unlikely instrument of deliverance could not be imagined. God wanted there to be no doubt that he was the facilitator of this miracle. When the world gives up on them, then God can begin to do His best work. Let the high and mighty reject God, He will go to the weak and beggarly souls. Luke 14:16-24 *"Then said he unto him, A certain man made a great supper, and bade many: And sent his servant at supper time to say to them that were bidden, Come; for all things are now ready. And they all with one consent began to make excuse. The first said unto him, I have bought a piece of ground, and I must needs go and see it: I pray thee have me excused. And another said, I have bought five yoke of oxen, and I go to prove them: I pray thee have me excused. And another said, I have married a wife, and therefore I cannot come. So that servant came, and shewed his lord these things. Then the master of the house being angry said to his servant, Go out quickly into the streets and lanes of the city, and bring in hither the poor, and the maimed, and the halt, and the blind. And the servant said, Lord, it is done as thou hast commanded, and yet there is room. And the lord said unto the servant, Go out into the highways and hedges, and compel them to come in, that my house may be filled. For I say unto you, That none of those men which were bidden shall taste of my supper."* God does not have to have me, I have to have Him. I can never forget where he brought me from.

It is truly a God moment when we realize what we are doing is not working. The lepers came to the realization that sitting there doing nothing was not working for them. It was time to get up and go to where the food was. We cannot just sit here expecting God to bring it to us. We must get up and do something. Your options may be limited but there is something that you can do. We cannot allow the trials of life to derail us. Ecclesiastes 2:22-23 *"For what hath man of all his labour, and of the vexation of his heart, wherein he hath laboured under the sun? For all his days are sorrows, and his travail grief; yea, his heart taketh not rest in the night. This is also vanity."* Theses laments from the book of Ecclesiastes are the endless words from the circle of life. They are the blueprints of life and show us what to expect: hope and disappointment, jubilation and failure, peace and despair, contentment and anger, love and hate, faith and fear. Spiritual complacency keeps the church from obtaining the Spiritual victory the Lord has for the church today. Let us examine some of the stumbling blocks that create a sense of spiritual complacency for many: unmovable objects, past failures, overwhelming odds, fear of the unknown, crushing losses and the success of the haughty. May the taste of the super natural we see in this lesson today create in us a hunger for the gifts of the spirit to be working in our churches.

Proverbs 28:1 *"The wicked flee when no man pursueth: but the righteous are bold as a lion."* When the Lord got done putting the squeeze on the Syrians, they run off leaving even the horses which would have made their escape quicker. The terrible thing about the guilt of sin is that man is always looking over his shoulder expecting the judgements of God to fall. No matter how many times you tell yourself that your sin is justified, you will never be able to get over the guilt of wrong doing. 1 Peter 3:20-21 *"Which sometime were disobedient, when once the longsuffering of God waited in the days of Noah, while the ark was a preparing, wherein few, that is, eight souls were saved by water. The like figure whereunto even baptism doth also now save us (not the putting away of the filth of the flesh, but the answer of a good conscience toward God,) by the resurrection of Jesus Christ."* It is only through baptism in the name of Jesus that our sins can be washed away and all the guilt and shame can be removed.

Pigs In The Parlor

> 2 Kings 7:8-14 *"And when these lepers came to the uttermost part of the camp, they went into one tent, and did eat and drink, and carried thence silver, and gold, and raiment, and went and hid it; and came again, and entered into another tent, and carried thence also, and went and hid it. 9 Then they said one to another, We do not well: this day is a day of good tidings, and we hold our peace: if we tarry till the morning light, some mischief will come upon us: now therefore come, that we may go and tell the king's household. 10 So they came and called unto the porter of the city: and they told them, saying, We came to the camp of the Syrians, and, behold, there was no man there, neither voice of man, but horses tied, and asses tied, and*

the tents as they were. 11 And he called the porters; and they told it to the king's house within. 12 And the king arose in the night, and said unto his servants, I will now shew you what the Syrians have done to us. They know that we be hungry; therefore are they gone out of the camp to hide themselves in the field, saying, When they come out of the city, we shall catch them alive, and get into the city. 13 And one of his servants answered and said, Let some take, I pray thee, five of the horses that remain, which are left in the city, (behold, they are as all the multitude of Israel that are left in it: behold, I say, they are even as all the multitude of the Israelites that are consumed:) and let us send and see. 14 They took therefore two chariot horses; and the king sent after the host of the Syrians, saying, Go and see.

We find the lepers walking into abundance and splendor with no thought of the source of their blessing. How easy it is to see others being blessed and then begin to criticize how they are using their blessings while doing nothing with what God has blessed you with. Matthew 7:3-6 *"And why beholdest thou the mote that is in thy brother's eye, but considerest not the beam that is in thine own eye? Or how wilt thou say to thy brother, Let me pull out the mote out of thine eye; and, behold, a beam is in thine own eye? Thou hypocrite, first cast out the beam out of thine own eye; and then shalt thou see clearly to cast out the mote out of thy brother's eye. Give not that which is holy unto the dogs, neither cast ye your pearls before swine, lest they trample them under their feet, and turn again and rend you."* They found more food than they could imagine and wealth for the picking. Like a pig in a parlor they begin to consume it upon their on lust. James 4:1-10 *"From whence come wars and fightings among you? come they not hence, even of your lusts that war in your members? Ye lust, and have not: ye kill, and desire to have, and cannot obtain: ye fight and war, yet ye have not, because ye ask not. Ye ask, and receive not, because ye ask amiss, that ye may consume it upon your lusts. Ye adulterers and adulteresses, know ye not that the friendship of the world is enmity with God? whosoever therefore will be a friend of the world is the enemy of God. Do ye think that the scripture saith in vain, The spirit that dwelleth in us lusteth to envy? But he giveth more grace. Wherefore he saith, God resisteth the proud, but giveth grace unto the humble. Submit yourselves therefore to God. Resist the devil, and he will flee from you. Draw nigh to God, and he will draw nigh to you. Cleanse your hands, ye sinners; and purify your hearts, ye double minded. Be afflicted, and mourn, and weep: let your laughter be turned to mourning, and your joy to heaviness. Humble yourselves in the sight of the Lord, and he shall lift you up."* Many times the reason we don't receive the blessing we pray for is because we cannot handle it. We are blessed to be a blessing. If we take the blessing and hoard all of them for ourselves they will become a curse.

Whether it was on their mother's knee or in a Sunday school class, the teaching of the past finally rose above the fog and the lepers realize they needed to share their bounty with those in need. Let me encourage the teachers today. I know you cry, pray and worry over the lessons you teach every week and go home wondering if anybody will retain anything that you said. We have this mighty promise about the effectiveness of the proclaimed Word of God. Isaiah 55:9-13 *"For as the heavens are higher than the earth, so are my ways higher than your ways, and my thoughts than your thoughts. For as the rain cometh down, and the snow from heaven, and returneth not thither, but watereth the earth, and maketh it bring forth and bud, that it may give seed to the sower, and bread to the eater: So shall my word be that goeth forth out of my mouth: it shall not return unto me void, but it shall accomplish that which I please, and it shall prosper in the thing whereto I sent it. For ye shall go out with joy, and be led forth with peace: the mountains and the hills shall break forth before you into singing, and all the trees of the field shall clap their hands. Instead of the thorn shall come up the fir tree, and instead of the brier shall come up the myrtle tree: and it shall be to the LORD for a name, for an everlasting sign that shall not be cut off."* We must remember that the Word of God is sometimes like the snow. We proclaim it and it just goes around the person but not in the person, just like the snow sits on top of the ground until the thaw comes. The time will come when the season in that persons' life will change and that word will begin to flow into their hearts.

When the lepers show up with a generous sample of their bounty the king is still clueless. In keeping with his past track record, he does not seek the counsel of the man of God. How in the world this stupid king came up with semi intelligent advisors is beyond me. It just had to be the mercy of God. But he finally listen to them and sent someone to check it out. How easy it is even today to miss the obvious when we are in the midst of a trail. I know that when your bags are packed and you mind is made up, the last thing you want to do is seek counsel from the man of God. But the proof is in the pudding, those who seek after the counsel of the man of God are shooting down the stream of blessings. Daniel 1:19-20 *"And the king communed with them; and among them all was found none like Daniel, Hananiah, Mishael, and Azariah: therefore stood they before the king. And in all matters of wisdom and understanding, that the king enquired of them, he found them ten times better than all the magicians and astrologers that were in all his realm."* These verses demonstrate how that Godly counsel is ten times better than anything you can find in the secular world.

The False Security Of Power And Intellect

2 Kings 7:15-20 "And they went after them unto Jordan: and, lo, all the way was full of garments and vessels, which the Syrians had cast away in their haste. And the messengers returned, and told the king. 16 And the people went out, and spoiled the tents of the Syrians. So a measure of fine flour was sold for a shekel, and two measures of barley for a shekel, according to the word of the LORD. 17 And the king appointed the lord on whose hand he leaned to have the charge of the gate: and the people trode upon him in the gate, and he died, as the man of God had said, who spake when the king came down to him. 18 And it came to pass as the man of God had spoken to the king, saying, Two measures of barley for a shekel, and a measure of fine flour for a shekel, shall be to morrow about this time in the gate of Samaria: 19 And that lord answered the man of God, and said, Now, behold, if the LORD should make windows in heaven, might such a thing be? And he said, Behold, thou shalt see it with thine eyes, but shalt not eat thereof. 20 And so it fell out unto him: for the people trode upon him in the gate, and he died."

Oh, did the Word of God ever come to pass. This was no vague prophecy of someone having a backache in the building. It was very specific, right down to the item and the price it would sell for. Don't be fooled by the false prophet telling you tall tales of blessing and giving some generic word to get the money out of your pocket. When God speaks, he will dot the I's and cross the T's. It is time for the gifts of the Spirit to flow in the endtime church. 1 Corinthians 12:28-31 *"And God hath set some in the church, first apostles, secondarily prophets, thirdly teachers, after that miracles, then gifts of healings, helps, governments, diversities of tongues. Are all apostles? are all prophets? are all teachers? are all workers of miracles? Have all the gifts of healing? do all speak with tongues? do all interpret? But covet earnestly the best gifts: and yet shew I unto you a more excellent way."* We will not have the miraculous working in our churches unless we are willing to seek after the gifts of the Spirit. I am not saying they will come easy, it will take a lot of prayer and dedication to have the gifts of the Spirit flowing in your church. The gifts of the Spirit are not a sensational side show but are the working of God to facilitate the redemption of mankind.

The lord of the king felt secure in his position of power and depended upon his intellect to provide him everything he so desired in life. What a rude awakening when the windows of heaven opened up and the abundance of food begin to flow into the city. How dangerous it is to mock the man of God. Before he could eat one chicken leg, the judgements of God fell and he was trampled to death. That which he depended upon did not save him from his judgement. As our world ricochets from one crisis to the next, they are learning they can no longer depend upon medical science, higher education, political leaders, careers, investments or family to deliver them out of their calamity. Proverbs 3:1-12 *"My son, forget not my law; but let thine heart keep my commandments: For length of days, and long life, and peace, shall they add to thee. Let not mercy and truth forsake thee: bind them about thy neck; write them upon the table of thine heart: So shalt thou find favour and good understanding in the sight of God and man. Trust in the LORD with all thine heart; and lean not unto thine own understanding. In all thy ways acknowledge him, and he shall direct thy paths. Be not wise in thine own eyes: fear the LORD, and depart from evil. It shall be health to thy navel, and marrow to thy bones. Honour the LORD with thy substance, and with the firstfruits of all thine increase: So shall thy barns be filled with plenty, and thy presses shall burst out with new wine. My son, despise not the chastening of the LORD; neither be weary of his correction: For whom the LORD loveth he correcteth; even as a father the son in whom he delighteth."*

Discussion Questions

1. What do we war against?

____

____

____

2. What are we to covet earnestly?

____

____

____

3. Who did God compel to come to the feast?

____

____

____

4. Why was the lord of the king trampled to death?

____

____

____

5. What does God do to the proud?

____

____

____

DOUBLE PORTION
The Miracles Of Elisha

Lesson Twelve

Double Famine

The double portion of Elisha is displayed in a unique way in the lesson today. We find that during the time of Elijah there was a great famine in the land that last for three and a half years. Luke 4:25-26 *"But I tell you of a truth, many widows were in Israel in the days of Elias, when the heaven was shut up three years and six months, when great famine was throughout all the land; But unto none of them was Elias sent, save unto Sarepta, a city of Sidon, unto a woman that was a widow."* The famine that happen during the time of Elisha lasted for seven years. So we see the famine during the time of Elisha lasted twice as long as the one during the time of Elijah. When God enlarges our borders, we also find that the giants that we battle will get larger. Jeremiah 12:5 *"If thou hast run with the footmen, and they have wearied thee, then how canst thou contend with horses? and if in the land of peace, wherein thou trustedst, they wearied thee, then how wilt thou do in the swelling of Jordan?"*

It is time to let the power of God move like it has never moved before. We are the endtime church and are going to fight devils that our grandparents never dreamed of fighting. Our greatest problems are no longer a pack of cigarettes or a woman in a short dress. We are fighting a spirit of perversion that is sweeping across our land and bringing mass confusion into the minds of young and old alike. They don't know if they are a boy or a girl.

161

They are glorifying pain and death. Morality is being trampled in the streets, Witchcraft and the occult is being openly displayed on their bodies. Mind altering drugs are being legalized on every corner. All kinds of unholy unions are being promoted. Pestilences and chaos is running rampant in the large cities. Romans 1:24-32 *"Wherefore God also gave them up to uncleanness through the lusts of their own hearts, to dishonour their own bodies between themselves: Who changed the truth of God into a lie, and worshipped and served the creature more than the Creator, who is blessed for ever. Amen. For this cause God gave them up unto vile affections: for even their women did change the natural use into that which is against nature: And likewise also the men, leaving the natural use of the woman, burned in their lust one toward another; men with men working that which is unseemly, and receiving in themselves that recompence of their error which was meet. And even as they did not like to retain God in their knowledge, God gave them over to a reprobate mind, to do those things which are not convenient; Being filled with all unrighteousness, fornication, wickedness, covetousness, maliciousness; full of envy, murder, debate, deceit, malignity; whisperers, Backbiters, haters of God, despiteful, proud, boasters, inventors of evil things, disobedient to parents, Without understanding, covenantbreakers, without natural affection, implacable, unmerciful: Who knowing the judgment of God, that they which commit such things are worthy of death, not only do the same, but have pleasure in them that do them."*

The reason Sodom and Gormorrha had these types of problems is because their pulpits were silent. Jude 1:7-16 *"Even as Sodom and Gomorrha, and the cities about them in like manner, giving themselves over to fornication, and going after strange flesh, are set forth for an example, suffering the vengeance of eternal fire. Likewise also these filthy dreamers defile the flesh, despise dominion, and speak evil of dignities. Yet Michael the archangel, when contending with the devil he disputed about the body of Moses, durst not bring against him a railing accusation, but said, The Lord rebuke thee. But these speak evil of those things which they know not: but what they know naturally, as brute beasts, in those things they corrupt themselves. Woe unto them! for they have gone in the way of Cain, and ran greedily after the error of Balaam for reward, and perished in the gainsaying of Core. These are spots in your feasts of charity, when they feast with you, feeding themselves without fear: clouds they are without water, carried about of winds; trees whose fruit withereth, without fruit, twice dead, plucked up by the roots; Raging waves of the sea, foaming out their own shame; wandering stars, to whom is reserved the blackness of darkness for ever. And Enoch also, the seventh from Adam, prophesied of these, saying, Behold, the Lord cometh with ten thousands of his saints, To execute judgment upon all, and to convince all that are ungodly among them of all their ungodly deeds which they have ungodly committed, and of all their hard speeches which ungodly sinners have spoken against him. These are murmurers, complainers, walking after their own lusts; and their mouth speaketh great swelling words, having men's persons in admiration because of advantage."* Not only are our enemies bigger but our portions of anointing and power is doubled over the generations of the past. The endtime church has the power that it needs to defeat all of these enemies and more.

We have no need to go hide in the corner, we are the victorious church that has been washed in the blood of the lamb. It is time for us to take this message into the highways and byways. We have the only message that will work, because we have the truth. The love of God that is in us will conquer any enemy we come up against. Romans 8:35-39 *"Who shall separate us from the love of Christ? shall tribulation, or distress, or persecution, or famine, or nakedness, or peril, or sword? As it is written, For thy sake we are killed all the day long; we are accounted as sheep for the slaughter. Nay, in all these things we are more than conquerors through him that loved us. For I am persuaded, that neither death, nor life, nor angels, nor principalities, nor powers, nor things present, nor things to come, Nor height, nor depth, nor any other creature, shall be able to separate us from the love of God, which is in Christ Jesus our Lord."*

Scripture Text

2 Kings 8:1-6 *"Then spake Elisha unto the woman, whose son he had restored to life, saying, Arise, and go thou and thine household, and sojourn wheresoever thou canst sojourn: for the LORD hath called for a famine; and it shall also come upon the land seven years. 2 And the woman arose, and did after the saying of the man of God: and she went with her household, and sojourned in the land of the Philistines seven years. 3 And it came to pass at the seven years' end, that the woman returned out of the land of the Philistines: and she went forth to cry unto the*

king for her house and for her land. 4 And the king talked with Gehazi the servant of the man of God, saying, Tell me, I pray thee, all the great things that Elisha hath done. 5 And it came to pass, as he was telling the king how he had restored a dead body to life, that, behold, the woman, whose son he had restored to life, cried to the king for her house and for her land. And Gehazi said, My lord, O king, this is the woman, and this is her son, whom Elisha restored to life. 6 And when the king asked the woman, she told him. So the king appointed unto her a certain officer, saying, Restore all that was hers, and all the fruits of the field since the day that she left the land, even until now."

2 Kings 8:7-15 *"And Elisha came to Damascus; and Benhadad the king of Syria was sick; and it was told him, saying, The man of God is come hither. 8 And the king said unto Hazael, Take a present in thine hand, and go, meet the man of God, and enquire of the LORD by him, saying, Shall I recover of this disease? 9 So Hazael went to meet him, and took a present with him, even of every good thing of Damascus, forty camels' burden, and came and stood before him, and said, Thy son Benhadad king of Syria hath sent me to thee, saying, Shall I recover of this disease? 10 And Elisha said unto him, Go, say unto him, Thou mayest certainly recover: howbeit the LORD hath shewed me that he shall surely die. 11 And he settled his countenance stedfastly, until he was ashamed: and the man of God wept. 12 And Hazael said, Why weepeth my lord? And he answered, Because I know the evil that thou wilt do unto the children of Israel: their strong holds wilt thou set on fire, and their young men wilt thou slay with the sword, and wilt dash their children, and rip up their women with child. 13 And Hazael said, But what, is thy servant a dog, that he should do this great thing? And Elisha answered, The LORD hath shewed me that thou shalt be king over Syria. 14 So he departed from Elisha, and came to his master; who said to him, What said Elisha to thee? And he answered, He told me that thou shouldest surely recover. 15 And it came to pass on the morrow, that he took a thick cloth, and dipped it in water, and spread it on his face, so that he died: and Hazael reigned in his stead."*

The Seven Year Famine

2 Kings 8:1 *"Then spake Elisha unto the woman, whose son he had restored to life, saying, Arise, and go thou and thine household, and sojourn wheresoever thou canst*

> *sojourn: for the LORD hath called for a famine; and it shall also come upon the land seven years."*

Over and over again the nation of Israel was chastised for their idol worship. The Prophet Ezekiel talks about the four sore judgements. Ezekiel 14:21 *"For thus saith the Lord GOD; How much more when I send my four sore judgments upon Jerusalem, the sword, and the famine, and the noisome beast, and the pestilence, to cut off from it man and beast?"* Once again the judgement of famine was coming upon the nation of Israel. Elisha had a divine revelation that this famine was going to last seven years. Many times when we see Elisha speaking what the Lord told him and doing the miraculous work of the Lord, he is referred to as the "man of God." When this title was used, it indicated that he was acting in his official capacity as the agent of God. So he went to the woman whose son he had restored to life, and instructed her to take a course of action that would protect her from the seven year famine.

A famine can come as the results of a prolong drought which will result in continual crop failure and drying up of the rest of the plant life. In a few cases famine has come as the results of incessant rains which had prevent the crops from being harvested. There are multiple ways the Lord could have provided for this woman during the famine. He could have provided rain for her fields while the others received no rain. He also could have caused her meal and oil to not run dry until it was over (1 Kings 17:16). But He chose to provide deliverance from another quarter this time. The method He chose to use gave her so much more than just a like cake to eat each day. This was not the first time Elisha had helped this Godly woman. She was one that regularly worshiped God at his gatherings. This goes to prove that God always takes care of his regular customers. Matthew 10:40-42 *"He that receiveth you receiveth me, and he that receiveth me receiveth him that sent me. He that receiveth a prophet in the name of a prophet shall receive a prophet's reward; and he that receiveth a righteous man in the name of a righteous man shall receive a righteous man's reward. And whosoever shall give to drink unto one of these little ones a cup of cold water only in the name of a disciple, verily I say unto you, he shall in no wise lose his reward."* When we are faithful to church and give honor to the man of God we will be rewarded.

Much Was Required

> 2 Kings 8:2 *"And the woman arose, and did after the saying of the man of God: and she went with her household, and sojourned in the land of the Philistines seven years."*

Even though the Lord did deliver the woman from the famine, the process was a severe test of her faith. She had to leave her home and property and take her possession and travel to a foreign land. The Lord had blessed her with great possession, so the transportation of those possession was a big ordeal. No matter which direction she would go, the inhabitants of the land held resentment and hostilities toward the children of Israel. She had to step out in faith believing that God would provide for her upon this journey. She regarded Elisha's message not like a friend giving a stock tip but as a message from God. She did not mummer or complain about her fate but with faith and trust in a man of God who had worked the miraculous in her life before, she traveled forward. Murmuring and complaining is an indicator of a person who is full of unbelief.

It is unfortunate that the territory of Judah did not open their doors to her for refuse. What a sad situation it is when strangers and sinners treat you with more kindness than so called Christians and family. We are blessed today to be a part of the family of God. It does not matter that our blood family turns their back on us because God has given us a new family that will be true. This world is not our home, we are just a passing through. This woman did not go to the land of the Philistines to live forever, she just sojourned there during the famine. When we go to church, we are at our home on earth amongst our family.

At The Appointed Time

> 2 King 8:3 *"And it came to pass at the seven years' end, that the woman returned out of the land of the Philistines: and she went forth to cry unto the king for her house and for her land."*

The Word of God does not tell us that she returned when the famine was over. It tells us that she returned at the end of the seven years. This is a testimony of someone who is faithful to the instructions of her man of God. Even King Saul got into major trouble with God when he disobeyed the instructions of the Prophet Samuel. On the surface it looked like he was doing a good thing. How could you fault someone for making a sacrifice to God? The problem was that the timing was off, he was to wait on the Prophet Samuel. 1 Samuel 15:22-23 *"And Samuel said, Hath the LORD as great delight in burnt offerings and sacrifices, as in obeying the voice of the LORD? Behold, to obey is better than sacrifice, and to hearken than the fat of rams. For rebellion is as the sin of witchcraft, and stubbornness is as iniquity and idolatry. Because thou hast rejected the word of the LORD, he hath also rejected thee from being king."* We do not want to get ahead of God and we do not want to fall behind. Timing is very important to God. When the man of God says it is not the time to do that right now, obey him and you will be blessed. Ecclesiastes 3:1-8 *"To every thing there is a season, and a time to every purpose under the heaven: A time to be born, and a time to die; a time to plant, and a time to pluck up that which is planted; A time to kill, and a time to heal; a time to break down, and a time to build up; A time to weep, and a time to laugh; a time to mourn, and a time to dance; A time to cast away stones, and a time to gather stones together; a time to embrace, and a time to refrain from embracing; A time to get, and a time to lose; a time to keep, and a time to cast away; A time to rend, and a time to sew; a time to keep silence, and a time to speak; A time to love, and a time to hate; a time of war, and a time of peace."* If all we ever do is sing and dance and never have preaching, we are missing God's timing.   If all we ever do is have teaching and preaching and never sing and dance, we are missing God's timing.

Who Will Be A Witness?

2 Kings 8:4-6 *"And the king talked with Gehazi the servant of the man of God, saying, Tell me, I pray thee, all the great things that Elisha hath done. 5 And it came to pass, as he was telling the king how he had restored a dead body to life, that, behold, the woman, whose son he had restored to life, cried to the king for her house and for her land. And Gehazi said, My lord, O king, this is the woman, and this is her son, whom Elisha restored to life. 6 And when the king asked the woman, she told him. So the king appointed unto her a certain officer, saying, Restore all that was hers, and all the fruits of the field since the day that she left the land, even until now."*

In 2 Kings chapter 5 we find Gehazi forsaking the Glory of God, so this event took place before that because Gehazi is called the servant of the man of God in this passage. Also a king would not have been talking to a leper and Jesus said that only Naaman was healed of leprosy during this time. It is a great thing that God had given Elisha favor with the king and he was will willing to hear of his exploits. Just like God gave Joseph favor and grace in the house of Potiphar. Genesis 39:3-4 *"And his master saw that the LORD was with him, and that the LORD made all that he did to prosper in his hand. And Joseph found grace in his sight, and he served him: and he made him overseer over his house, and all that he had he put into his hand."* God gives you favor so that you can be a witness. Every day we need to be looking for an opportunity to witness to our family, friends, co-workers, neighbors and people we do business with about the miraculous power of the Holy Ghost. When is the last time you invited someone to church?

Who had taken possession of her property and why they would not give it back is not explained here. But we do see a child of God stepping forth to seek justice. She was not sitting back and expecting God to do something that she could do for herself. In the book of Galatians we find a paradox. Galatians 6:2-5 *"Bear ye one another's burdens, and so fulfil the law of Christ. For if a man think himself to be something, when he is nothing, he deceiveth himself. But let every man prove his own work, and then shall he have rejoicing in himself alone, and not in another. For every man shall bear his own burden."* How can I bear my brother's burden when he is commanded to bear his own burden? After further study we come to understand that we are to help our brother once he has proven that his burden if too heavy for him at the moment. But as soon as he is able, he is to pick it up again and bear it.

There are many that want to hear of the wonderful miracles of the Kingdom of God. They want you to pray for them and tell them of the goodness of the Lord. But they do not walk on with God. Even the Apostle Paul had a king who heard his preaching but did not accept it. Acts 26:26-28 *"For the king knoweth of these things, before whom also I speak freely: for I am persuaded that none of these things are hidden from him; for this thing was not done in a corner. King Agrippa, believest thou the prophets? I know that thou believest. Then Agrippa said unto Paul, Almost thou persuadest me to be a Christian."* What is it that would cause someone so close the miraculous to turn their back and go the other way?

Where Did Elisha Go During The Famine?

> 2 Kings 8:7-8 *"And Elisha came to Damascus; and Benhadad the king of Syria was sick; and it was told him, saying, The man of God is come hither. 8 And the king said unto Hazael, Take a present in thine hand, and go, meet the man of God, and enquire of the LORD by him, saying, Shall I recover of this disease?"*

The Prophet Elisha also left Samaria and sojourned to a distant land during the famine. We also find that during the famine that happened to King Ahab and Queen Jezebel that the Prophet Elijah went to Cherith and then to Zarephath. Now the judgements of God are raining down on Samaria and the man of God is removed from them. There comes a point after people have rejected God that He begins to remove everything holy and blessed from their life. One of the great torments of Hell is going to be the total absence of God's holy presence. 2 Thessalonians 1:8-9 *"In flaming fire taking vengeance on them that know not God, and that obey not the gospel of our Lord Jesus Christ: Who shall be punished with everlasting destruction from the presence of the Lord, and from the glory of his power."* There will only be the presence of evil in Hell. Sixty seconds out of every minute, sixty minutes out of every hour, twenty four hours out of every day, three hundred and sixty five days out of every year, it will be nothing but evil spirts tormenting the mind with all the opportunities you missed to live for God. 2 Peter 2:4-6 *"For if God spared not the angels that sinned, but cast them down to hell, and delivered them into chains of darkness, to be reserved unto judgment; And spared not the old world, but saved Noah the eighth person, a preacher of righteousness, bringing in the flood upon the world of the ungodly; And turning the cities of Sodom and Gomorrha into ashes condemned them with an overthrow, making them an ensample unto those that after should live ungodly."* Who are we to think that God would allow us to thumb our noses at his commandments and escape Hell?

Those who do not reject God have a promise that he will keeps his messenger speaking into their life. Isaiah 30:20-21 *"And though the Lord give you the bread of adversity, and the water of affliction, yet shall not thy teachers be removed into a corner any more, but thine eyes shall see thy teachers: And thine ears shall hear a word behind thee, saying, This is the way, walk ye in it, when ye turn to the right hand, and when ye turn to the left."* Without the Holy Ghost filled teachers, we would be groping in the darkness, tripping and falling over ever obstacle. We thank God for Holy Ghost filled preachers who will keep on preaching to us even when we are doing wrong and don't want to hear it.

Damascus is one of the oldest cities in the Middle East. It is on the crossroad between Asia and Africa. It had over 100 monuments constructed during its history. Damascus covers the northwestern part of a beautiful and fruitful plain. This plain is intersected by numerous mountain streams. The stream Nahr Barada separates into seven branches upon leaving the mountains, two of which pass through Damascus. The rich vegetation of the plain as well as the numerous gardens behind which the city lies, conceals the city to the traveler approaching from the desert. Damascus existed during the time of Abraham (Genesis 14:15). Paul started his ministry in Damascus (Acts 9:19 -22).

During the reign of Kind Ahab and Queen Jezebel, King Benhadad was defeated by them. They spared his life and he made a covenant with them. 1 Kings 20:31,34 *"And his servants said unto him, Behold now, we have heard that the kings of the house of Israel are merciful kings: let us, I pray thee, put sackcloth on our loins, and ropes upon our heads, and go out to the king of Israel: peradventure he will save thy life. 34 And Benhadad said unto him, The cities, which my father took from thy father, I will restore; and thou shalt make streets for thee in Damascus, as my father made in Samaria. Then said Ahab, I will send thee away with this covenant. So he made a covenant with him, and sent him away."* So by this covenant, Elisha had the right to live in Damascus.

All the nations during that time would seek the advice of their prophets when there was serious illness in the family. When King Jeroboam's son was seriously ill he had his wife inquire of the Prophet Ahijah what was to become of the child. (1 Kings 14:1- 12). King Ahaziah had an accident that proved fatal, he sent messengers to inquire of Baalzebub the god of Ekron. (2 Kings 1:1-6). King Behadad had already learned that the idols of his land were powerless before the God of Israel.   1 Kings 20:27-30 *"And the children of Israel were numbered, and were all present, and went against them: and the children of Israel pitched before them like two little flocks of kids; but the Syrians filled the country. And there came a man of God, and spake unto the king of Israel, and said, Thus saith the LORD, Because the Syrians have said, The LORD is God of the hills, but he is not God of the valleys, therefore will I deliver all this great multitude into thine hand, and ye shall know that I am the LORD. And they pitched one over against the other seven days. And so it was, that in the seventh day the battle was joined: and the children of Israel slew of the Syrians an hundred thousand footmen in one day. But the rest fled to Aphek, into the city; and there a wall fell upon twenty and seven thousand of the men that were left. And Benhadad fled, and came into the city, into an inner chamber."* So when he wanted to know if he was going to live or die, he sent a messenger to the Prophet Elisha, the prophet of the most powerful God he had ever encountered.   Unfortunately he did not ask the prophet to come and pray for him. His only concern was for his body, with no concern for his eternal destination. We need to note that many times after Jesus healed someone he would tell them to go and sin no more.   The healing was designed to give them an opportunity to live for God. God does not heal so that we may continue in sin.

The No And Yes Answer

> 2 Kings 8:9-10 *"So Hazael went to meet him, and took a present with him, even of every good thing of Damascus, forty camels' burden, and came and stood before him, and said, Thy son Benhadad king of Syria hath sent me to thee, saying, Shall I recover of this disease? 10 And Elisha said unto him, Go, say unto him, Thou mayest certainly recover: howbeit the LORD hath shewed me that he shall surely die."*

We see a pattern of people bringing a gift to the prophet when they enquired of him. Saul expressed discomfort because he did not have a gift to bring unto the prophet. 1 Samuel 9:6-7 *"And he said unto him, Behold now, there is in this city a man of God, and he is an honourable man; all that he saith cometh surely to pass: now let us go thither; peradventure he can shew us our way that we should go. Then said Saul to his servant, But, behold, if we go, what shall we bring the man? for the bread is spent in our vessels, and there is not a present to bring to the man of God: what have we?"* Namaan brought a millions dollars' worth of gifts when he came to the Prophet Elisha to be healed (2 Kings 5:5). Why would we come to the house of the Lord and not bring an offering? 2 Corinthians 9:6-7 *"But this I say, He which soweth sparingly shall reap also sparingly; and he which soweth bountifully shall reap also bountifully. Every man according as he purposeth in his heart, so let him give; not grudgingly, or of necessity: for God loveth a cheerful giver."* What blessing are given to those whom God loveth. Go ahead and hang on to it if you want too. Haggai 1:5-6 *"Now therefore thus saith the LORD of hosts; Consider your ways. Ye have sown much, and bring in little; ye eat, but ye have not enough; ye drink, but ye are not filled with drink; ye clothe you, but there is none warm; and he that earneth wages earneth wages to put it into a bag with holes."* It will become like a canker that rotteth the soul. The Lord shows Elisha that King Benhadad illness was not terminal and so he told Hazael that he could recover from the illness. But the rest of the story was that King Benhadad was going to be assassinated. Elisha was in a touchy situation here, he had to answer the unasked question and reveal to Hazael the darkness of his heart. Time is the child of God friend. In time all the hidden will be brought to light. Luke 12:2-3 *"For there is nothing covered, that shall not be revealed; neither hid, that shall not be known. Therefore whatsoever ye have spoken in darkness shall be heard in the light; and that which ye have spoken in the ear in closets shall be proclaimed upon the housetops."*

Weeping Over Lost Opportunities

2 Kings 8:11-13 *"And he settled his countenance stedfastly, until he was ashamed: and the man of God wept. 12 And Hazael said, Why weepeth my lord? And he answered, Because I know the evil that thou wilt do unto the children of Israel: their strong holds wilt thou set on fire, and their young men wilt thou slay with the sword, and wilt dash their children, and rip up their women with child. 13 And Hazael said, But what, is thy servant a dog, that he should do this great thing? And Elisha answered, The LORD hath shewed me that thou shalt be king over Syria."*

Hazeal tried to conceal the fact that he was elated that his plan to assassinate King Benhadad was going to succeed. But there was still the God given conscience that brought shame to his face when he realized that the prophet knew of his murderous intent. God knows the thoughts and intent of the heart. How tragic it is when evil intent is reveal and mankind tries to cover it up. Hebrews 4:12-13 *"For the word of God is quick, and powerful, and sharper than any twoedged sword, piercing even to the dividing asunder of soul and spirit, and of the joints and marrow, and is a discerner of the thoughts and intents of the heart. Neither is there any creature that is not manifest in his sight: but all things are naked and opened unto the eyes of him with whom we have to do."* You cannot fool God and ultimately you cannot fool the man of God. Your true intentions will be revealed to the man of God. We are living in a day when our society has loss respect for the ministry. I remember as a boy going to town with my dad and everyone we meet in town would greet my dad as a "Reverend." We are still required to give honor to our Pastor. We show respect because we are respectable. 1 Timothy 5:17 *"Let the elders that rule well be counted worthy of double honour, especially they who labour in the word and doctrine."*

On this occasion though the weeping was not over the murderous evil that Hazael was about to do, it was for the children of Israel. God has revealed to the Prophet Elisha that Hazael was going to inflict unimaginable horrors upon the rebellious children of Israel. Just as Jesus weep over Jerusalem because they were going to reject truth and keep their traditions. Luke 13:34 *"O Jerusalem, Jerusalem, which killest the prophets, and stonest them that are sent unto thee; how often would I have gathered thy children together, as a hen doth gather her brood under her wings, and ye would not!"* I cannot count the tears I have shed over rebellious saints. They would buck up with pride and dare God or the preacher to condemn them. It does not bring the preacher joy to see sons and daughters lose their fathers, husbands to kill their wives, babies die in the crib, houses to burn down, mothers to go crazy, cars to explode, unexplainable illness to strike the healthy, a young person destroy their future or dozens of other judgements of God that I have experienced.

Where Will You Be When You Get Where Your Going?

2 Kings 8:14-15 *"So he departed from Elisha, and came to his master; who said to him, What said Elisha to thee? And*

he answered, He told me that thou shouldest surely recover. 15 And it came to pass on the morrow, that he took a thick cloth, and dipped it in water, and spread it on his face, so that he died: and Hazael reigned in his stead."

Just as Jesus foretold of the betrayal of Judas and did nothing to stop him, Elisha does nothing to deter of dissuade Hazael of his murderous intent. God knew the evil in the heart of Hazael and knew if revealing his heart did not stop him, nothing would. God is not going to hit you between the eyes with a two by four, he is just going to warn you. It is sad to see someone ignore the warning of God or think they can just have a little fun and then run back to the safety of the church. How naive are the youth of our day thinking they are going to play with sin and not get bitten. Proverbs 7:24-27 *"Hearken unto me now therefore, O ye children, and attend to the words of my mouth. Let not thine heart decline to her ways, go not astray in her paths. For she hath cast down many wounded: yea, many strong men have been slain by her. Her house is the way to hell, going down to the chambers of death."* When you allow evil to enter into your heart it will drag you down into the miry clay. How deceived our world is today, all thinking that they are basically a good person. Without the Holy Ghost in control in our lives, we all have the potential to be the next serial killer.

Hazael delivered Elisha's message by holding back the most important part. Many lies are just partial truth delivered in a way to make you believe it is the whole truth. Today in pulpits all over our nation, false prophets are delivering messages of partial truth. They try to convince man that all they must do to be saved is believe on Jesus. This is a partial truth and when proclaimed as the total truth becomes a lie. On the birthday of the church when the lost ask the Apostle Peter what they must do to be saved he told them the whole truth. Acts 2:37-40 *"Now when they heard this, they were pricked in their heart, and said unto Peter and to the rest of the apostles, Men and brethren, what shall we do? Then Peter said unto them, Repent, and be baptized every one of you in the name of Jesus Christ for the remission of sins, and ye shall receive the gift of the Holy Ghost. For the promise is unto you, and to your children, and to all that are afar off, even as many as the Lord our God shall call. And with many other words did he testify and exhort, saying, Save yourselves from this untoward generation."*

Discussion Questions

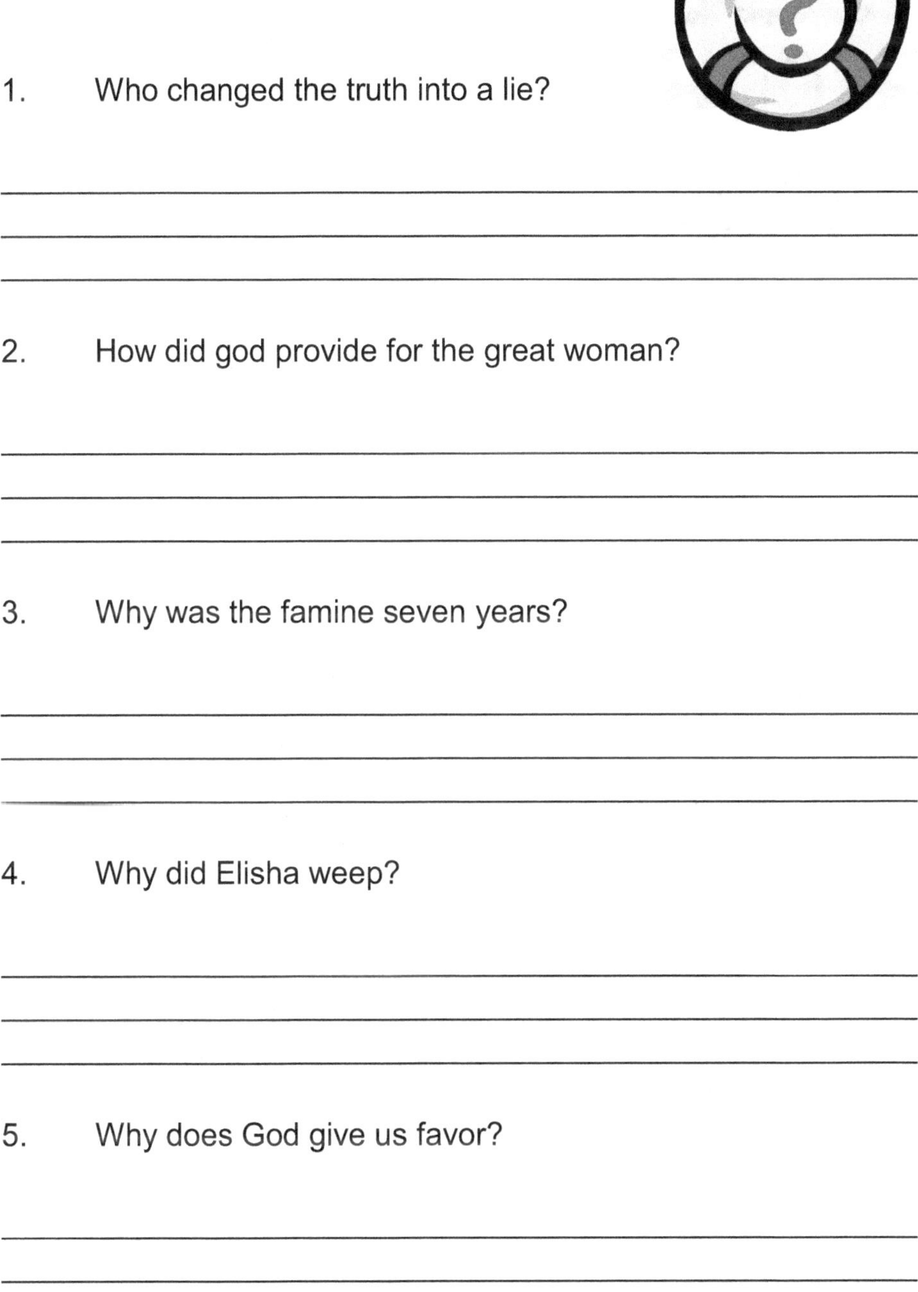

1.   Who changed the truth into a lie?

2.   How did god provide for the great woman?

3.   Why was the famine seven years?

4.   Why did Elisha weep?

5.   Why does God give us favor?

Double Portion
The Miracles Of Elisha

Lesson Thirteen

Empty Shoes

When a legend makes their last curtain call, we are left feeling defenseless and deprived. We know that life will never be the same. That pillar of strength and wisdom has been bulldozed over and the future now has so many uncertainties. Who are we going to call? Where are we going to receive that word of wisdom. What will hold our group together? Do we know which direction to go? Will our enemies attack us now that we are venerable? Who will show the next generation the old paths? Will the ancient landmarks be forgotten? What does the future hold? How can we replicate the success of the past?

We have certain milestones that we cross in life that will cause us to contemplate what will be done with our fields of labor when we pass them on. So many of us begin with nothing and fought and scratched a work out of the dirt. We prayed and fasted and went without to see the work of the Lord go forward. The sleepless nights and buckets of tears we shed did not stop us, we got up in the morning and went back to war. The friends that betrayed us along the way left us feeling wounded for many years. The help we received along the way was scarce and scant. We had the Sanballts and Tobiahs come by and laugh us to scorn, telling everyone we would amount to nothing. Nehemiah 4:1-3 *"But it came to pass, that when Sanballat heard that we builded the wall, he was wroth, and took great indignation, and mocked the Jews. And he spake before his brethren and the army of Samaria, and said, What do these feeble Jews? will they fortify themselves? will they sacrifice? will they make an end in a day? will they revive the stones out of the heaps of the rubbish which are burned? Now Tobiah the Ammonite was by him, and he said, Even that which they build, if a fox go up, he shall even break down their stone wall."* We stuck it out and lived for God and made a difference for the Kingdom of God. We have been blessed and have something to show for our labor of love. But the day will come when we must pass it on. When we look around us and see what has happen to others when they passed the fields of labor to a new shepherd, we are racked with concern. We are not alone, the wisest man that ever lived, King Solomon, became very concerned that all of his labors would be wasted by his successor. Ecclesiastes 2:18-19 *"Yea, I hated all my labour which I had taken under the sun: because I should leave it unto the man that shall be after me. And who knoweth whether he shall be a wise man or a fool? yet shall he have rule over all my labour wherein I have laboured, and wherein I have shewed myself wise under the sun. This is also vanity."* We have seen the riches of so many squandered by their ungrateful successors. Who will be able to fill our EMPTY SHOES?

Scripture Text

2 Kings 13:14-21 *"Now Elisha was fallen sick of his sickness whereof he died. And Joash the king of Israel came down unto him, and wept over his face, and said, O my father, my father, the chariot of Israel, and the horsemen thereof. 15 And Elisha said unto him, Take bow and arrows. And he took unto him bow and arrows. 16 And he said to the king of Israel, Put thine hand upon the bow. And he put his hand upon it: and Elisha put his hands upon the king's hands. 17 And he said, Open the window eastward. And he opened it. Then Elisha said, Shoot. And he shot. And he said, The arrow of the LORD'S deliverance, and the arrow of deliverance from Syria: for thou shalt smite the Syrians in Aphek, till thou have consumed them. 18 And he said, Take the arrows. And he took them. And he said unto the king of Israel, Smite upon the ground. And he smote thrice, and stayed. 19 And the man of God was wroth with him, and said, Thou shouldest have smitten five or six times; then hadst thou smitten Syria till thou hadst consumed it: whereas now thou shalt smite Syria but*

thrice. 20 And Elisha died, and they buried him. And the bands of the Moabites invaded the land at the coming in of the year. 21 And it came to pass, as they were burying a man, that, behold, they spied a band of men; and they cast the man into the sepulchre of Elisha: and when the man was let down, and touched the bones of Elisha, he revived, and stood up on his feet."

The End Of An Age

2 Kings 13:14 *"Now Elisha was fallen sick of his sickness whereof he died. And Joash the king of Israel came down unto him, and wept over his face, and said, O my father, my father, the chariot of Israel, and the horsemen thereof."*

The Word of God does not tell us how old Elisha was at his death. But when we total up the years the various kings lived and reigned and what prophets he worked with, we conclude that he was a very old man. It is very likely that he was ninety plus years old at the time the Lord took him home. The things the Lord was able to accomplish with him, even though he had no political power or priestly position is astounding. He walks onto the stage working and walks off the stage doing the same. He typified the servant's heart. In Paul's parting words to the church at Ephesus, he told them that he had taught them everything he could, and it was up to them now to sink or swim. Acts 20:32-38 *"And now, brethren, I commend you to God, and to the word of his grace, which is able to build you up, and to give you an inheritance among all them which are sanctified. I have coveted no man's silver, or gold, or apparel. Yea, ye yourselves know, that these hands have ministered unto my necessities, and to them that were with me. I have shewed you all things, how that so labouring ye ought to support the weak, and to remember the words of the Lord Jesus, how he said, It is more blessed to give than to receive. And when he had thus spoken, he kneeled down, and prayed with them all. And they all wept sore, and fell on Paul's neck, and kissed him, Sorrowing most of all for the words which he spake, that they should see his face no more. And they accompanied him unto the ship."*

Many times we do not value something until we are about to lose it. It was not the custom of kings to visit dying people in the Middle East. The nation of Israel was still in rebellion against God and King Joash did not fear the Lord. This visit by King Joash indicates that Elisha had not spent his last years living in idleness and pursuits of relaxation and entertainment. He had been active in the ministry and was a force to be reckoned with. There was no doubt in the king's mind that the power of God still worked through him. He had to have known of the many times that Elisha had saved the nation of Israel from destruction. King Joash came to Elisha with fear gripping his heart and tears of hopelessness in his eyes. He knew that Elisha would be dead soon and that the King Hazael of Syria was coming to conquer his nation. What was he going to do? .

The Arrow Of Deliverance

> 2 Kings 13:15-17 *"And Elisha said unto him, Take bow and arrows. And he took unto him bow and arrows. 16 And he said to the king of Israel, Put thine hand upon the bow. And he put his hand upon it: and Elisha put his hands upon the king's hands. 17 And he said, Open the window eastward. And he opened it. Then Elisha said, Shoot. And he shot. And he said, The arrow of the LORD'S deliverance, and the arrow of deliverance from Syria: for thou shalt smite the Syrians in Aphek, till thou have consumed them."*

The status of his visitor did not impress Elisha. He went right to work telling the king what he must do. Too many people are impressed with money and power and cannot be used of God to bring instruction unto the lives of the rich and famous. We must remember that God is no respecter of persons. It does not matter how much money you have in the bank or how much fame you may claim, you must be born again in order to enter the Kingdom of God. The gifts of God cannot be bought with money. Acts 8:18 -20 *"And when Simon saw that through laying on of the apostles' hands the Holy Ghost was given, he offered them money, Saying, Give me also this power, that on whomsoever I lay hands, he may receive the Holy Ghost. But Peter said unto him, Thy money perish with thee, because thou hast thought that the gift of God may be purchased with money."* We should never give preferential treatment to people because of their ability to give great sums of money to the church. It is not about the sum of money that we give, it is about whether of not that the giving is a sacrifice. If we only give to get the recognition of man, we have lost our blessing. Mark 12:41-44 *"And Jesus sat over against the treasury, and beheld how the people cast money into the treasury:*

and many that were rich cast in much. 4And there came a certain poor widow, and she threw in two mites, which make a farthing. And he called unto him his disciples, and saith unto them, Verily I say unto you, That this poor widow hath cast more in, than all they which have cast into the treasury: For all they did cast in of their abundance; but she of her want did cast in all that she had, even all her living." Please observe that Jesus does pay attention to what we give to the Kingdom of God. The more we give, the more we will be blessed. God will bless the sacrificial giver.

In order for the king to receive from God what he wanted, he must be willing to take part in this symbolic gesture. If he had not been willing to take the bow and shoot the arrow out the window there would not have been a miracle for him. Even today some people do not understand why we lay hands on the sick and anoint them with oil. James 5:14-15 *"Is any sick among you? let him call for the elders of the church; and let them pray over him, anointing him with oil in the name of the Lord: And the prayer of faith shall save the sick, and the Lord shall raise him up; and if he have committed sins, they shall be forgiven him."* The power is not in the oil, nor is it in the hand of a man. The power is in the name of Jesus which comes when this symbolic gesture is carried out by qualified ministers of the Gospel over an individual with faith. We also see in this same vein of ministry the anointing of handkerchiefs with oil, praying over them in the name of Jesus, then the handkerchiefs working miraculous healing for believers. Acts 19:11-12 *"And God wrought special miracles by the hands of Paul: So that from his body were brought unto the sick handkerchiefs or aprons, and the diseases departed from them, and the evil spirits went out of them."*

Just as Jesus told parables to the people to illustrate his message and put mud in the blind man's eyes before he healed them, we use visual illustration (similitudes) in our preaching and teaching today. The Word of God tells us that he uses these visual illustration to speak to his people. Hosea 12:10 *"I have also spoken by the prophets, and I have multiplied visions, and used similitudes, by the ministry of the prophets."* Let us not be lazy in our presentation of the Gospel. Let us use the gifts and talents that God has given us to communicate the Gospel to every creature. Break your material down to the level of the person you are teaching. You do not want to choke them with meat. Give them the milk of the Word until they are able to handle the meat. Hebrews 5:11-14 *"Of whom we have many things to say, and hard to be uttered, seeing ye are dull of hearing. For when for the time ye ought to be teachers, ye have need that one teach you again which be the first principles of the oracles of God; and are become such as have need of milk, and not of strong meat. For every one that useth milk is unskilful in the word of righteousness: for he is a babe. But strong meat belongeth to them that are of full age, even those who by reason of use have their senses exercised to discern both good and evil."* Let us have a passion for the Word of God so that we may grow and be able to teach others also. Just like a baby does not have teeth and cannot eat meat, neither will you have the knowledge to teach the Word of God overnight. Your growth in the Lord will be determined by how much of the Word of God you consume.

King Joash had to be willing to allow the man of God to direct his hands before he could be used as a deliverer of Israel. The attitude of so many of our youth today is that they can find their own way. They resent anyone trying to direct their hands. They allow their limited exposure and fantasy identity to give them a false sense of security. How much more can we do when we stand on the shoulders of the giants that have come before us? Jeremiah 6:16-17 *"Thus saith the LORD, Stand ye in the ways, and see, and ask for the old paths, where is the good way, and walk therein, and ye shall find rest for your souls. But they said, We will not walk therein. Also I set watchmen over you, saying, Hearken to the sound of the trumpet. But they said, We will not hearken."* Let us not sacrifice our children to the demonic entertainment industry. There is a reason that the old timers have set a standard against the polluting of our children's minds with exposure to cussing, drinking, immorality, nudity, immodest clothing, lying, stealing, abuser of themselves (Romans 1:22-32), creature worship, witchcraft, demonic music, and the mocking of Christians. Until the youth allow the elders to direct their hand, they will never experience the miraculous. Don't ever confuse sensationalism for the miraculous.

Even the direction the arrow was to be shot had meaning. The arrow was not to be shot in just any old direction. But in order for it to be an arrow of deliverance it had to be directed at the land in bondage. 2 Kings 10:32-33 *"In those days the LORD began to cut Israel short: and Hazael smote them in all the coasts of*

Israel; From Jordan eastward, all the land of Gilead, the Gadites, and the Reubenites, and the Manassites, from Aroer, which is by the river Arnon, even Gilead and Bashan." We need to catch the vison of the Pastor of this church in order to see the chains of darkness broken in our community. Put aside your pet little project and get aboard the deliverance train of this church. The starving children in India need help but that is not your mission until the Lord gives that vison unto your Pastor. Acts 16:4-10 *"And as they went through the cities, they delivered them the decrees for to keep, that were ordained of the apostles and elders which were at Jerusalem. And so were the churches established in the faith, and increased in number daily. Now when they had gone throughout Phrygia and the region of Galatia, and were forbidden of the Holy Ghost to preach the word in Asia, After they were come to Mysia, they assayed to go into Bithynia: but the Spirit suffered them not. And they passing by Mysia came down to Troas. And a vision appeared to Paul in the night; There stood a man of Macedonia, and prayed him, saying, Come over into Macedonia, and help us. And after he had seen the vision, immediately we endeavoured to go into Macedonia, assuredly gathering that the Lord had called us for to preach the gospel unto them."*

The Endurance Test

> 2 Kings 13:18-19 *"And he said, Take the arrows. And he took them. And he said unto the king of Israel, Smite upon the ground. And he smote thrice, and stayed. 19 And the man of God was wroth with him, and said, Thou shouldest have smitten five or six times; then hadst thou smitten Syria till thou hadst consumed it: whereas now thou shalt smite Syria but thrice."*

Once again we see the term the "Man of God" used here to designate that Elisha is being used in his official capacity as the prophet of Israel to perform a miracle. What was it that caused King Joash to stop smiting the ground? Maybe if we consider the operations of a GPS on our phone we will get some insight into his problem. We pull up one of the GPS apps on our phone and type in a destination and tap get directions. The GPS begins to talk to us and tell us to turn or go straight. There are time it is frustrating because we don't understand how to carry out it instructions. Other times there is too much traffic and we miss our exit and it goes through that whole recalculating routine. There is never a good place to turn around when you need it. Then we finally get on the right road and it shuts up. It does not say, "You are an awesome driver, keep it up." There is no comments about how boring it is to drive on the same road for 200 miles. You do not get a reminder to take a bathroom break. As long as you are on the right road and there is no change in direction coming up, it is silent. God is that way sometimes. He tells us what to do and as long as we are doing a good job, He is silent. Unfortunately our human nature can get weary in well doing. We want change and do not realize that change will undermine the miraculous that God is performing in our lives. We must wait and care for the precious fruit before it can come to harvest.

I was recently going to preach for a friend who had a new church and was not real familiar with where it was located. So I set one GPS app to the city the church was in and had it start giving me directions. As I got closer to the church I decided to put the exact address into my GPS app. What I did not realize was that I had chosen a different app for the exact address. When I rolled into town both apps begin talking to me. The spiritual lesson came when I was about four blocks from the church. One GPS app told me to turn right and the other GPS app told me to turn left. Now I had competing voices in my ear and had to figure out which one was telling me the truth. 1 Corinthians 14:7-12 *"And even things without life giving sound, whether pipe or harp, except they give a distinction in the sounds, how shall it be known what is piped or harped? For if the trumpet give an uncertain sound, who shall prepare himself to the battle? So likewise ye, except ye utter by the tongue words easy to be understood, how shall it be known what is spoken? for ye shall speak into the air. There are, it may be, so many kinds of voices in the world, and none of them is without signification. Therefore if I know not the meaning of the voice, I shall be unto him that speaketh a barbarian, and he that speaketh shall be a barbarian unto me. Even so ye, forasmuch as ye are zealous of spiritual gifts, seek that ye may excel to the edifying of the church."* The time has come for us to filter out all the others voices and listen to the voice of our under shepherd, the Pastor of this church. Your Pastor is ordained of God to give the church direction so they may make heaven their home.

King Joash stopped short of total victory. If he would just have endured a little longer he would have achieved total victory. There are several reasons that we can become weary. We can be disappointed in the current results we are experiencing. We can lose sight of our destination. We can forget about the reward that we will receive upon completion. We can begin to doubt that the victory is obtainable. One of the easiest to succumb to is the gossip of the idle hands. 2 Thessalonians 3:11-15 *"For we hear that there are some which walk among you disorderly, working not at all, but are busybodies. Now them that are such we command and exhort by our Lord Jesus Christ, that with quietness they work, and eat their own bread. But ye, brethren, be not weary in well doing. And if any man obey not our word by this epistle, note that man, and have no company with him, that he may be ashamed. Yet count him not as an enemy, but admonish him as a brother."* Here we are busting our cans and the lazy bums are getting all of the attention and recognition. It doesn't seem fair, but time is your friend, they will wither away but your work will build a memorial.

I want you to know that you can have complete and total victory. Just winning the battle for today is not the best results. We need to win some battles once and for all. It is time to defeat that enemy and never have to face that trial again. Let us pass this test so we can move up to the next level. I am afraid there is many in the church who are stopping short of what they might become. We do not press on and reach to that which God wants us to obtain. Philippians 3:12-20 *"Not as though I had already attained, either were already perfect: but I follow after, if that I may apprehend that for which also I am apprehended of Christ Jesus. Brethren, I count not myself to have apprehended: but this one thing I do, forgetting those things which are behind, and reaching forth unto those things which are before, I press toward the mark for the prize of the high calling of God in Christ Jesus. Let us therefore, as many as be perfect, be thus minded: and if in any thing ye be otherwise minded, God shall reveal even this unto you. Nevertheless, whereto we have already attained, let us walk by the same rule, let us mind the same thing. Brethren, be followers together of me, and mark them which walk so as ye have us for an ensample. (For many walk, of whom I have told you often, and now tell you even weeping, that they are the enemies of the cross of Christ: Whose end is destruction, whose God is their belly, and whose glory is in their shame, who mind earthly things.) For our conversation is in heaven; from whence also we look for the Saviour, the Lord Jesus Christ."*

We have the best weapon possible to win the victory with. Don't go to war with a butter knife when you can have the atomic bomb. Learn about your arsenal so that you might be equipped with the weapons of victory. Ephesians 6:10-18 *"Finally, my brethren, be strong in the Lord, and in the power of his might. Put on the whole armour of God, that ye may be able to stand against the wiles of the devil. For we wrestle not against flesh and blood, but against principalities, against powers, against the rulers of the darkness of this world, against spiritual wickedness in high places. Wherefore take unto you the whole armour of God, that ye may be able to withstand in the evil day, and having done all, to stand. Stand therefore, having your loins girt about with truth, and having on the breastplate of righteousness; And your feet shod with the preparation of the gospel of peace; Above all, taking the shield of faith, wherewith ye shall be able to quench all the fiery darts of the wicked. And take the helmet of salvation, and the sword of the Spirit, which is the word of God: Praying always with all prayer and supplication in the Spirit, and watching thereunto with all perseverance and supplication for all saints."*

The End Was Not The End

> 2 Kings 13:20-21 *"And Elisha died, and they buried him. And the bands of the Moabites invaded the land at the coming in of the year. 21 And it came to pass, as they were burying a man, that, behold, they spied a band of men; and they cast the man into the sepulchre of Elisha: and when the man was let down, and touched the bones of Elisha, he revived, and stood up on his feet."*

He did not get an exit in a chariot of fire but the distinct honor the Lord bestowed upon him was miraculous and unique. Even though man had forgotten the faithfulness of Elisha, God did not forget it and chose to honor him after death with a miracle. This is a type and shadow of the resurrection of Jesus Christ. The resurrection of Jesus brings new life to all believers and the bones of Elisha brought new life to one man. Your prayer will continue to be answered after your death. It is never too late to pray. Keep praying for your lost family members, those prayers will build a memorial before God. Acts 10:3-4 *"He saw in a vision evidently about the ninth hour of the day an angel of God coming in to him, and saying unto him, Cornelius. And when he looked on him, he was afraid, and said, What is it, Lord? And he said unto him, Thy prayers and thine alms are come up for a memorial before God."*

The Sons of the Prophets are never mentioned again. Elisha invested in and used many prophets to help him do the work of the Lord. Why did none of them step up and carry on the work he was doing? It is not till the Prophet Isaiah arrives that we see a Prophet perform another miracle. Moses was the only Old Testament prophet which the Word of God records doing more miracles than Elisha. Deuteronomy 34:10-12 *"And there arose not a prophet since in Israel like unto Moses, whom the LORD knew face to face, In all the signs and the wonders, which the LORD sent him to do in the land of Egypt to Pharaoh, and to all his servants, and to all his land, And in all that mighty hand, and in all the great terror which Moses shewed in the sight of all Israel."* Elisha, Elijah, Moses and David were all called the "man of God" multiple times. But very few of the other prophets were given that honor. Timothy in the New Testament was given the honor of being called the "man of God." If we are willing today to preach the truth, we too can have that honor. 2 Timothy 3:13-17 *"But evil men and seducers shall wax worse and worse, deceiving, and being deceived. But continue thou in the things which thou hast learned and hast been assured of, knowing of whom thou hast learned them; And that from a child thou hast known the holy scriptures, which are able to make thee wise unto salvation through faith which is in Christ Jesus. All scripture is given by inspiration of God, and is profitable for doctrine, for reproof, for correction, for instruction in righteousness: That the man of God may be perfect, throughly furnished unto all good works."*

Who will pick up the mantle of anointing as the legends of today walk off the stage? Too many of them are laying discarded while the stage of talent and popularity is full. We must continue to work hard as we prepare the next generation to accept the mantle of anointing. How precious is the anointing of the Lord and we don't want to see one drop of it wasted. We must never forget the elders who blazed a trail before us. They are not just a tombstone in a graveyard, they are holy men of God who gave all that we may have the fresh anointing flowing through our churches today. I am determined that their work will not become discarded items in the yard sale of history. You must look yourself in the face and declare, I WILL FILL THOSE EMPTY SHOES.

Twelve Parallels Between Elisha And Jesus.

1.   **Their names have similar meanings.**

   a.   Elisha means "God is salvation."
   b. Jesus means "Jehovah has become salvation."

2.   **Their ministries started at the Jordan River.**

   a.   Elisha takes up the mantle of Elijah at the Jordan River and becomes the prophet of Israel.
   b.   Jesus is baptized by John at the Jordan River and starts teaching and preaching.

   c.   Elisha sees the heavens open and Elijah being taken up in a whirlwind and then receives a double portion.
   d.   At Jesus' baptism John sees the heavens open and the Spirit descend.

3.   **They both raised a woman's son from the dead.**

   a.   Elisha raises the son of the Shunaammite woman from the dead.
   b.   Jesus raises the son of the widow of Nain from the dead.

4,   **They both feed large parties by multiplying the food.**

   a.   Elisha feeds 100 prophets with a few barley loaves and there is food left over.
   b.   Jesus, on two occasions, feeds 5000 and then 4000 with a few loaves and fishes and there is food left over.

5.   **They both turn a small quantity of liquid into enough to meet the need.**

   a.   Elisha turns a small amount of oil into enough oil to fill many vessels.
   b.   Jesus turns water into huge quantities of wine.

6.   **They both healed lepers.**

a. Elisha heals the Syrian commander Naaman of leprosy.
b. Jesus heals many lepers.

7. They are both betrayed over money.

a. Elisha is betrayed by Gehazi because he sees an opportunity to make money.
b. Jesus is betrayed by Judas because he sees an opportunity to get money.

8. They both made things float.

a. Elisha makes an iron axe head float.
b. Jesus walks on water and enables his disciple Peter to walk (float) on water.

9. They both gave sight to the blind.

a. Elisha first blinds the Syrians and then restores their sight.
b. Jesus often restored the sight of the blind.

10. They both wept over the nation of Israel.

a. Elisha wept over Israel when he was in Damascus.
b. Jesus wept over Israel.

11. They both appeared before a king.

a. Elisha appeared before King Jehoram.
b. Jesus appeared before King Herod.

12. After their deaths they bring new life.

a. Enemy soldiers interrupted a burial and the body was thrown quickly into Elisha's tomb and upon touching Elisha's bones the dead man came back to life.
b. Jesus was raised to life and brought the promise of new birth to all mankind.

Discussion Questions

1. Why should we leave our labors to a wise man?

____

____

____

2. How can we successfully minister in our retirement years?

____

____

____

3. Why was the man of God wroth with King Joash?

____

____

____

4. What is total victory?

____

____

____

5. How important is it to teach the next generation?

____

____

____

Messages From The Book Of Acts

QUARTERLY BIBLE STUDY

Tom Akers

AFF
Publications
www.affp.1church4u.com

AFF
Publications
www.affp.1church4u.com

www.ingramcontent.com/pod-product-compliance
Lightning Source LLC
Chambersburg PA
CBHW071416150726
48000CB00001B/347